YOGA
and The Body of Christ

DAVE HUNT

The Berean Call

BEND • OREGON

YOGA AND THE BODY OF CHRIST:
WHAT POSITION SHOULD CHRISTIANS HOLD?

Published by The Berean Call
Copyright © 2006

ISBN: 1-928660-48-7
ISBN-13: 978-1-928660-48-4

Unless otherwise indicated, Scripture quotations are from
The Holy Bible, King James Version (KJV)

Some material for this volume is derived from
Occult Invasion by Dave Hunt (out of print)
Harvest House Publishers, ISBN 1-56507-269-3

The Berean Call
PO Box 7019
Bend, Oregon, 97708-7019

Printed in the United States of America

CONTENTS

–1–

WHAT ABOUT YOGA?

Yogi Bhajan died October 6, 2004. On April 5 and 6, 2005, respectively, the U.S. House and Senate unanimously passed a joint resolution praising this deceased Sikh leader for his "teachings...about Sikhism and yoga...." Yoga is at the very heart of Hinduism, and Sikhism is similar to a "denomination" within Hinduism.

On May 11, 2005, a special reception was held at the U.S. Capitol commemorating the Congressional Resolution. It was attended by "U.S. Senators and Representatives, members of the U.S. Department of State, representatives from the Government of India, dignitaries, officials, and members of the Sikh faith...." The news release declared that Yogi Bhajan improved the lives of thousands "through his teachings on yoga and Sikh Dharma."[1] The founder of the 3HO (Healthy, Happy, Holy) organization taught that these three qualities of life could be realized through practicing yoga. (We document the far different sordid truth in Chapter 6.)

The foundation of Bhajan's yogic technique was the "Sa-Ta-Na-Ma" mantra repeated in a precise way during daily yoga practice: "projected mentally from the back top of the head, down, and then straight out the third eye point...between the eyebrows at the root of the nose.... Using this technique," said Yogi Bhajan, "you can know the Unknown and see the Unseen. If you spend two hours per day in meditation, God will meditate on you the rest of the day."[2] We have, of course, only his word that such a claim is true.

In contrast to the advertisements promoting yoga in the West today, this statement says nothing about physical benefits—yoga was not designed for that. It is all about getting in touch with "god." Indeed, the purpose is to achieve the realization that each individual practicing yoga *is* god. And no less a government authority than Congress gives its enthusiastic official approval of Yogi Bhajan and his initiation of thousands into supposed godhood through his brand of yoga!

Why the Anti-Christian Prejudice?

What about "the separation of church and state" that Congress and the Supreme Court usually enforce so vigorously? One soon discovers that in America this restriction seems to apply only to the Bible and Christianity. The United States was once known as a "Christian nation." Today, it could well be called an "anti-Christian nation." Christian symbols, such as the Cross or the Ten Commandments, may not be displayed in public places. Yet the American Congress quite openly supports and honors Sikhism—to say nothing of Islam, which both political and religious leaders continually praise as a "religion of peace" at official functions. (For the truth about Islam, see *Judgment Day* by this author.)

The fact that Jesus Christ physically resurrected (as testified by many eyewitnesses), left behind an empty tomb, and promised to return bodily to earth one day, is apparently not sufficient to qualify Him for public honor by the U.S. government. But because Yogi Bhajan declared, "When I'll be physically gone, search me out spiritually. You'll have to sit together to do it,"[3] he is somehow qualified for special public honors from the United States government itself.

Perhaps the crucial difference is that Yogi Bhajan (like the revered Tibetan spiritual leader, the Dalai Lama) practiced and promoted yoga, while Jesus Christ did not. As we shall see, however, increasing numbers of those who call themselves Christians are claiming that Jesus did indeed teach and practice yoga after all. Perhaps they are hoping that if He could be accepted as a yogi along with the god-men of India and Tibet, Christmas celebrations would no longer be banned from public schools and manger scenes and crosses from public display.

Buddhism, Hinduism, Islam, native American Indian paganism, shamanism—anything and anyone except Christianity and Jesus Christ are highly honored and can be promoted in our public schools. The U.S. Post Office made a special Eid stamp to commemorate the feast that ends Ramadan; and American presidents, including George W. Bush, hold dinners in the White House in honor of Islam's "holy month [and] great faith...."[4] And the ACLU makes no objection. They would go all the way to the Supreme Court to prevent the same honor being given to Jesus Christ! This is the national climate in which the practice of yoga has grown so rapidly.

Can Yoga Be Purely Physical?

That non-Christians are engaging in yoga is not surprising. After all, it is being promoted in the West as purely physical stretching and breathing exercises beneficial for one's health—even as a cure for cancer, with testimonials that supposedly back up that claim. That Christians, however, who say they follow Christ and His Word, would also jump on the bandwagon of Eastern mysticism is staggering.

Yoga was developed to escape this "unreal" world of time and sense and to reach *moksha*, the Hindu heaven—or to return to the "void" of the Buddhist. With its breathing exercises and limbering-up positions, yoga is promoted in the West for enhancing health and better *living*—but in the far East, where it originated, it is understood to be a way of *dying*. Yogis claim to possess the ability to survive on almost no oxygen and to remain motionless for hours, free of the "illusion" of this life. The physical aspects of yoga, however, which attract many Westerners, were, in fact, originally developed and practiced for spiritual goals.

In spite of the widely published fact that yoga comes from occult practices in such places as China, India, and Tibet, and was not designed to enhance health but to achieve godhood, it is still popularly believed that one can engage in it strictly for health reasons and without any religious or spiritual involvement. John Patrick Sullivan, former NFL player and current yoga instructor in Santa Barbara, California, declares, "Yoga has no religion. It's not about Hinduism [or] Buddhism...."[5] Such opinions, however, are contradicted by original practitioners of yoga and by all of the experts who know it best.

Swiss psychiatrist C. G. Jung, who was heavily involved in the occult and not a Christian by any means, was one of the pioneers in bringing yoga to the West 85 years ago and remained devoted to it all of his life. He declared authoritatively and emphatically that the spiritual cannot be cut out of yoga:

> The numerous purely physical procedures of yoga [unite] the parts of the body...with the whole of the mind and spirit, as...in the pranayama exercises, where prana is both the breath and the universal dynamics of the cosmos... the elation of the body becomes one with the elation of the spirit.... Yoga practice is unthinkable, and would also be ineffectual, without the ideas on which it is based. It works the physical and the spiritual into one another in an extraordinarily complete way. [6]

What Jung declared is stated no less explicitly by yogic sages in the East, where this system originated. Nevertheless, that fact is still widely denied by most yoga instructors in the West. Thus, the popularity and practice of this Eastern occult technique for uniting the spirit of man with the Universal Spirit (Hinduism's chief god, Brahman) continues to explode in the Western world. And it does so under the guise of being purely physical in spite of overwhelming evidence to the contrary.

The following is from a popular yoga website, which seeks to explain what yoga really is. Note the contradiction of "scientific teaching...based on Hindu philosophy," spirituality without religion, and the ecumenism of Hinduism, which has a "universal spirit" that is allegedly compatible with all religions:

> *What is Yoga?* Yoga literally means union. It is the practical and scientific teaching, including a system of exercises for attaining bodily and mental control and well-being that

aims at bringing about the union of the human spirit with the universal spirit.

Is Yoga a Religion? No, although yoga is an Indian tradition and more or less based on Hindu philosophy, it does not belong to any particular region or religion. Its practical and scientific techniques work effectively regardless of a person's belief. [7]

Non-Religious Practices

Such mind-numbing contradictions are overlooked when it comes to anything except Christianity. True biblical Christianity is continually under fire from all sides, but any other "faith" (including a false and ecumenical "Christianity") is accepted no matter how absurd and contradictory its doctrines and practices. Consider the following: "The heart of the true Hindu goes out to the Man on the cross, who exclaimed even at that hour, Father! Forgive them; for they know not what they do! The true Hindu is all admiration for the great Prophet of Arabia [Muhammad] who literally transformed a barbaric People into a well-knit moral society. But he can never tolerate the small-minded fanatics who try to pooh-pooh every other faith."[8]

Irrational though it may be, it is acceptable that all religions are embraced by Hinduism and deemed to be compatible with one another and with yoga even though they contradict one another on the most basic points. Hinduism has more than 300 million gods; Islam declares that Allah is "the only God;" and Buddhism is basically atheistic—yet they are all embraced by the yogi. All major religions claim to honor "Christ," yet all deny Christ's claims about Himself.

Evangelical Christians are "small-minded fanatics" because they believe Christ's declaration: "I am the way, the truth, and the life: no man cometh unto the Father, but by me" (John 14:6). In their zeal to "extol" Jesus along with every other "prophet," "true Hindus" reject what He actually declared in the most direct terms. This is neither rational nor honest! And this ecumenical double-talk even claims that Jesus himself taught and practiced yoga. For that absurd claim, there is not one scintilla of biblical or historical evidence—but that fact seems to trouble no yoga enthusiast.

Basketball coach Phil Jackson was applauded for turning the Chicago Bulls' headquarters into a sacred repository of fetishes and totems and introducing his entire team to Eastern mysticism. *Newsweek* referred favorably to Jackson as the man "who brought Zen principles to bear in coaching the Chicago Bulls to three consecutive NBA championships." The article lauded Jackson for accomplishing "one of the more daunting challenges in the history of religion."[9]

It would have been another story had he indoctrinated his team with Christianity. Had that occurred, it would have been soundly condemned by the media and the NBA. Yet this discriminatory abuse of Christianity, this blatant prejudice against the biblical Christ, is approved, while Christians who seek to follow Christ and to be true to His clear teachings are maligned as narrow-minded.

The laws in "Christian" America have almost completely banned Christianity from public arenas. Yet at the same time, all other religions are accepted. This almost universal attitude is not only irrational but reveals a deep prejudice against Christianity that begs an explanation. "Me thinkest thou protesteth too loudly" certainly applies in this case. Such universal protest, which at times becomes hateful, vicious, and violent, and has produced not only the crucifixion of Christ but literally millions of Christian martyrs through the centuries, can hardly be a chance reaction. There must be some purpose and power behind it!

A Massive Missionary Endeavor

Hindu gurus from the East, such as Maharishi Mahesh Yogi, Baba Muktananda, Yogananda, Yogi Bhajan, Vivekananda, and a host of others, were pleased to learn in the late '50s and early '60s, that through the popular use of psychedelic drugs, millions of Westerners were experiencing a nonphysical reality that Western science had long denied existed. They were quick to recognize that a vast market for their teachings had thereby been opened up in the West. The New Age movement was birthed. Yoga, once practiced in the East only by "holy men," was made available to the masses in the West, and it soon spread everywhere, even into churches and among evangelicals.

The call went out to Hindus and yoga enthusiasts, "The New Age movement...has accepted the great ideas of the East.... Let us invade the American Campuses armed with the vision of Vedanta."[10] Few, if any, realized that the West had fallen victim to the largest and most successful missionary campaign in history.

Missionary campaign? Most Westerners find it difficult to think of these smiling, bowing, obsequious, and supposedly broadminded yogis, swamis, and lamas as missionaries determined to spread their mystic gospel. It comes as a great surprise that the largest missionary organization in the world is not Christian but Hindu—India's Vishva Hindu Parishad (VHP). Of course, that's acceptable to the media and the world—only Christian missionaries are held in contempt and maligned.

Yes, Hindus have launched the largest missionary effort in

history. Nearly thirty years ago, in January 1979, at the VHP-sponsored second "World Congress on Hinduism" in Allahabad, India, attended by about 60,000 delegates from around the world, a speaker declared, "Our mission in the West has been crowned with fantastic success. Hinduism is becoming the dominant world religion, and the end of Christianity has come near." By law, no Christian missionary activity is allowed among Hindus in India, but Hindu missionaries aggressively evangelize the West—and with great success. Among the primary goals listed in VHP's constitution are the following:

> To establish an order of missionaries, both lay and initiate, [for] the purpose of propagating dynamic Hinduism representing...various faiths and denominations, including Buddhists, Jains, Sikhs, Lingayats, etc., and to open, manage or assist seminaries or centers for spiritual principles and practices of Hinduism...in all parts of the world....[11]

Foremost among the "centers for spiritual principles and practices of Hinduism" in the West are the ever-multiplying places where yoga is taught. Interestingly, the 1979 World Hindu conference was chaired by the Dalai Lama, who publicly and dishonestly proclaims tolerance for all religions. Hinduism and Buddhism, both of which advocate similar yoga practices, infiltrate our society, government, and even public schools as *science*, while Christianity is banned as a *religion*. Does the Dalai Lama practice and propagate yoga? Of course!

The VHP has branches all over the world. The umbrella organization in the United States is called Vishwa Hindu Parashad of America, Inc. It has its own website and carries on its missionary activities in cooperation with various gurus. For example, there is an annual Vivekananda Family Camp at which the typical day begins, "with yoga and meditation at 7 AM." In 1992, the VHP of America launched "World Vision 2000" to carry Swami Vivekananda's message based on Vedanta to America.[12]

The "God-man" Honored by the World

Of all the gurus who have come to the West, none has done more to establish the credibility of Eastern mysticism than Tenzin Gyatso, the Dalai Lama, spiritual leader in exile of Tibet's Gelugpa, or Yellow sect, of Mahayana Buddhism. He claims to be the fourteenth reincarnation of the original Dalai Lama, a god on earth with the power to initiate others into their own godhood. Here, we have again the persistent occult theme of human deification echoing the Serpent's lie in the Garden of Eden ("Ye shall be as gods" – Genesis 3:5)—and that goal is the heart of all yoga, in spite of the protests that it is non-religious.

The Dalai Lama travels the world, initiating huge admiring and trusting audiences, including tens of thousands of Westerners, into "Tibetan Tantric Deity Yoga." He promises initiates that they will become Bodhisatvas (little Buddhas), realizing their inherent godhood and able to create their own reality. For initiating multitudes into his brand of yoga (through the "Kalachakra ritual for world peace," accompanied by the traditional Tibetan "Sand Mandala"), he was given the Nobel Peace Prize in 1989. Ten years earlier, on his first visit to the United States, "His Holiness" was welcomed to St. Patrick's Cathedral in New York City, where his statement that "all the world's religions are basically the same" was rewarded with a standing ovation by the naïve and trusting overflow (mostly Roman Catholic) crowd.[13] The Dalai Lama was also welcomed as he preached to a no-less-attentive and appreciative audience from the pulpit of the cathedral in

Geneva, Switzerland, where John Calvin once held forth.

In August 1996, Hollywood elites, such as actor Richard Gere and MGM President Mike Marcus, honored the Dalai Lama at a fund-raising dinner for the American Himalayan Foundation. The thousand guests contributed about $650,000. Harrison Ford introduced the self-proclaimed god. Of course, Shirley MacLaine (crawling farther out on that limb) was on hand, along with Leonard Nimoy and many other well-known celebrities.

A number of Hollywood movies have been made related to the Dalai Lama's escape from Tibet and his life's work worldwide. At the annual Hollywood Film Festival in 2004, the prize for "Best Documentary" was awarded to *What Remains of Us*, shot clandestinely inside Tibet. It depicts the story of a Tibetan refugee who carried a video message to Tibet from the Dalai Lama for her people, and shows the excitement of Tibetans secretly watching it. Interestingly, Hollywood seeks to tell the "true story" of the lives of the Dalai Lama or Muhammad but does not grant such a courtesy to Jesus Christ. It portrays Him in a variety of the most outrageously false and demeaning ways. This deep prejudice cannot be denied and begs an explanation.

A Worldwide Deceit

As part of the most massive missionary effort in history—directly intended to destroy Christianity—every guru who has come to the West (from Maharishi Mahesh Yogi to Bhagwan Shri Rajneesh to Baba Muktananda) was sent here by his guru specifically to win converts to a Hindu/Buddhist pantheistic faith. Yogananda, for example, came to spread the teachings of his spiritual guru, Sri Babaji. Maharishi was sent to the West by his guru Dev and initiated millions into his TM brand of yoga. Yet the missionaries from the East all protest that they are teaching the *science* of yoga, health, and higher states of consciousness, *not religion*—and they are believed and highly honored for this deceit.

We can register no legitimate complaint against those who seek to persuade others of what they sincerely believe to be important truth. However, they should not lie about their product or purpose. And that is exactly what the gurus from the East have done. The magnitude of this deceit would be comparable to the Pope in his travels claiming that, instead of heading a church, he represented a group of secular scientists.

India banned foreign missionaries shortly after it gained independence. At the same time, however, India's missionaries travel the world, converting millions to Hinduism and Buddhism while protesting their tolerance for all religions and denying the religious nature of their mission. The fact that the media promotes such deception should be disturbing to any fair-minded person. It ought to be even more troubling to learn the suppressed facts that we intend to provide in the following pages. And yet rarely is an eyebrow raised, because very few know the facts or seem to care.

There has been much criticism, some of it no doubt justified, of Western missionaries who have gone to Africa, China, India, and other places, with the gospel of Jesus Christ and have attempted to westernize other cultures. Westernization of any culture cannot be justified and has nothing to do with Christianity, which itself (from Abraham to the Apostle Paul) began in the Middle East. In fairness, however, we must ask why there has been little or no criticism of Buddhist, Hindu, and Muslim missionaries who have aggressively pushed their religion and their way of life upon a willingly deceived Western world.

But What about Hatha Yoga?

Most Westerners imagine that Hatha Yoga (often called "physical yoga") has nothing to do with Hinduism or spirituality. Isn't at least *this* form of yoga purely physical? If that is the case, one is compelled to ask why, for example, in Chicago the center for Hatha Yoga instruction is located in the "Temple of Kriya Yoga," which for decades "has been a leader in providing high-quality, in-depth training for those who aspire to teach Yoga." Instructors are trained under the direction of "Sri Goswami Kriyanandaji [who] carries the Flame of the Lineage of Sri Babaji, brought to this country by Paramahansa Yogananda."[14]

The fact that the West was ready to adopt yogic spirituality under the guise of health enhancement was thoroughly demonstrated by Paramahansa Yogananda. This pioneer Hindu missionary founded the "Self-Realization Society," with headquarters in Southern California. Not counting the multitudes initiated by his followers, Yogananda personally initiated some 100,000 into the practice of Kriya Yoga (also known as Hatha Yoga) for the express purpose of "self-realization." Today there are millions of Americans who practice Hatha Yoga under the illusion that it is purely physical and has nothing to do with spirituality or religion. This is a popular and deeply entrenched delusion deliberately promoted among unsuspecting Westerners.

If Hatha Yoga is purely physical, why has it been handed down from "spiritual masters" known as yogis? Why is authentic Hatha Yoga always associated with spiritual meditation aimed at "self-realization" (i.e., to "realize one's oneness with 'God,' as Hinduism teaches")? If there are centers in the West that claim to offer a purely physical Hatha Yoga for health benefits alone, why do they teach the very same breathing exercises and positions that Paramahansa Yogananda brought to the West from India as taught to him by his spiritual guru, Sri Babaji? These techniques were all precisely developed over centuries to induce subtle changes in states of consciousness leading to "self-realization." They were not developed primarily for physical benefits.

If they are honest, the instructors of Hatha Yoga themselves, even in the West, admit that it is *not* purely physical. Richard Hittleman, one of the early pioneers of this so-called "physical" yoga in America, stated that "as yoga students practiced the physical positions, they would eventually be ready to investigate the spiritual component which is 'the entire essence of the subject.'"[15] Such is the consensus of the experts. Concerning Hatha Yoga, well-known teacher of yoga, Swami Sivenanda Radha, declared: "Asanas (physical postures and exercises) are a devotional practice...each asana creates a certain state of mind...to bring the seeker into closer contact with the Higher Self."[16] And by "higher self," of course, they mean whatever you want to accept as the "god within and without."

Yoga was introduced by Lord Krishna in the *Bhagavad Gita* as the sure way to Hindu heaven; and Shiva (one of the most feared Hindu deities, known as "The Destroyer") is addressed as *Yogeshwara*, Lord of Yoga. One of the most authoritative Hatha Yoga texts, the fifteenth-century *Hathayoga-Pradipika* by Svatmarama, lists Lord Shiva as the first Hatha Yoga teacher. The average yoga instructor never mentions (and may not even know) the many warnings in ancient texts that "Hatha Yoga is a dangerous tool. One can be possessed by a Hindu deity (i.e., demon) through the altered state of consciousness induced by this practice."

If what Western yoga teachers offer merely involves physical stretching and breathing exercises, as they claim, why don't they promote it only as such? Why do they persist in calling it "yoga," while denying any connection to what yoga really is? Why this cover-up?

We ignore at our peril the truth about yoga confessed by those who know it best—a truth that we intend to pursue in the following pages.

1. http://www.sikhnet.com/s/CongressHonor.

2. Sri Singh Sahb Bhai Sahib Harbhajan Singh Khalsa Yogiji, *The Teachings of Yogi Bhajan* (New York: Hawthorn Books, 1977), 4.

3. http://www.kundaliniyoga.com/clients/ikyta/webshell.nsf/WebParentNavLookup/62DB48EF3856D82287256A090079DC7A?OpenDocument.

4. http://whitehouse.gov/news/releases/2004/11/20041110-9.html.

5. *Santa Barbara News Press*, January 15, 2006.

6. C. G. Jung, trans. R.F.C. Hull, *Psychology and the East* (Princeton University Press, 1978), 80-81.

7. http://psychology.about.com/library/weekly/aa041503a.htm.

8. http://www.hindubooks.org/wehwk/chapter18/page1.htm.

9. Jerry Adler, "800,000 Hands Clapping," in *Newsweek*, June 13, 1994, 46.

10. http://www.hindunet.org/vivekananda/gk_gv2000.

11. Dave Hunt and T. A. McMahon, *The Sorceror's New Apprentice* (Eugene, OR: Harvest House Publishers, 1988), 281.

12. http://www.hindunet.org/vivekananda/gk_gv2000.

13. *Time*, September 17, 1979, 96.

14. http://www.yogakriya.org/about.htm.

15. *Yoga Journal*, May/June 1993, 68.

16. http://cana.userworld.com/cana_yoga.html.

—2—

ЧOGA FOR CHRISTIANS?

The fact that Christians are now practicing yoga in increasing numbers is puzzling in view of widely published warnings (many by yogis themselves, as well as by former yoga instructors) concerning its occult roots and attendant dangers, both spiritual and emotional. Astonishingly, there are about 586,000 references on "Google Search" under the heading of "Yoga for Christians." When one enters "Christian churches and yoga," the response lists 512,000 references! Of course, not all are favorable, but this shows the growing scope of interest and influence.

Could this be one more sign of the apostasy that Christ (as well as Paul and other apostles) warned would characterize the Last Days just before our Lord's return to catch up His own out of this world to heaven in an event known as the Rapture? Or is yoga, as even some Christian leaders are now claiming, a biblical approach to God that was actually taught and practiced by Christ and the early church but because of prejudice was not recognized as such for 1,900 years by evangelicals? If so, why doesn't the word "yoga" appear even once in the Bible, and why are there no references in its pages to anyone engaging in any practice even remotely related?

Even Hindus recognize the error in trying to "Christianize" yoga. In response to the fact that "Christian yoga is a growing fitness craze," Subhas Tiwari, a professor at the Hindu University of America in Orlando, Florida, said, "Hinduism is at yoga's core." Noting that yoga was practiced 3,000 years before the birth of Christ, mostly in India, Tiwari comments, "If you give me a recipe and I alter the ingredients...and give it back to you, am I giving you the same thing? Clearly not."[1]

The total lack of biblical support seems not to trouble Christians practicing yoga—and that is not a good sign. Is this fact related to Paul's solemn warning that in the last days "some shall depart from the faith, giving heed to seducing spirits, and doctrines of devils..." (1 Timothy 4:1)? Of course, many Christians are not yet ready to disregard Scripture, but such a willingness seems to be gathering momentum.

Consider a well-known Baptist Church in Memphis, Tennessee, which offered classes in the practice of yoga in 2001. Shortly after the first announcement appeared in the church bulletin, staff members began to receive complaints from members who were concerned about yoga's Eastern origins in Hinduism, Buddhism, and Taoism. But that concern was soon replaced by acceptance and growing enthusiasm.

"We got a little bit of flak for it," admitted the recreation ministry programmer. She quickly added that her church had carefully avoided any of yoga's Eastern philosophy elements, adopting only its "quiet, gentle, stretching exercise" aspects—an impossible naïveté, according to many experts. She explained that the church only promoted "Christian yoga as an exercise and relaxation tool." By the fall of 2003, it was "one of the most popular classes at the church, served up four days a week."[2] Apparently, yoga had become more popular than Bible study or Christ himself.

Who Is Deceiving Whom?

"Christian yoga"? How could that be? The falseness of such an idea should be clear from the fact that yoga originated long before Christ was born, and He certainly never practiced, taught, or commended it. Neither the apostles nor the early church engaged in yoga. One cannot just adopt a religious practice and call it Christianity. This faith was "once [for all] delivered to the saints," and believers everywhere and at all times are exhorted to "earnestly contend" for it (Jude 3). It is therefore dishonest to introduce some new element—particularly something like yoga, which comes from Hinduism—and call it "Christian."

The truth is that the entire idea of "Christian yoga" has neither biblical nor historical basis but is of very recent origin. Scripture warns: "To the law and to the testimony: if they speak not according to this word, it is because there is no light in them" (Isaiah 8:20). If the Word of God is no longer the Christian's guide, what kind of "Christianity" could the practice of yoga be?

Yoga originated in India as part of the paganism practiced there. How and when could it have become "Christian"? Obviously, it couldn't have, because the Bible clearly teaches that Jesus Christ is "the same yesterday, and today, and forever" (Hebrews 13:8). Moreover, the biblical God declares, "I...the Lord change not" (Malachi 3:6). Those who teach and practice "Christian yoga" must have therefore departed from Scripture. Nevertheless, the church in Memphis is not the only one making such an unbiblical claim. Newspaper notices such as the following are becoming more common: "Martha Johnson is coordinating FYC (Faith Yoga Class) at Grace Covenant Presbyterian Church. The classes are held at 9:30 a.m. Mondays and Wednesdays, 6:30 p.m. Thursdays, and 9 a.m. Saturdays."[3]

The First Baptist Church in Jackson, Mississippi, has been offering classes in "Christian Yoga" at its Christian Life Center for four years. These classes were begun by Susan Mason, who was featured in the film, *The Fire of Yoga*. In her classes, "Mason integrates Christian spirituality into a physical art with Hindu roots [embracing] the practice that helped heal her body and spirit after debilitating cancer treatments."[4] What could possibly be wrong with something apparently so beneficial? Yet according to the Bible, "Christian spirituality" is totally *spiritual* and has nothing to do with physical exercises. Nor could Christianity have any relationship whatsoever to Hinduism, which is, in fact, its diametric opposite.

Nevertheless, Mason first encountered "Christian" yoga seven years earlier in "a therapeutic yoga class at Jackson's Baptist Hospital to help heal from cancer.... Mason sees no conflict between yoga and Christianity.... 'There's a lot of correlation between yoga philosophy and Christian philosophy,' she said. 'A lot has to do with man's search for spirituality.'"

On the contrary, Christianity does not involve a "search for spirituality." The Christian has been born of the Spirit of God into the family of God. The Christian's concern is to allow the Spirit of Christ, who has come to indwell his spirit, to express the very *life* of Christ, through faith, ever more fully in the believer's own life, thus deepening that relationship.

In defending yoga against the claim that it comes from Eastern religion, Mark Oestreicher of Youth Specialties argues, "Christianity *is* an Eastern religion. It has all its roots in the East...."[5] In response to criticism for having yoga each morning at the National Pastors Conference sponsored by Youth Specialties, Oestreicher said, "Yoga is really just about stretching and slowing down. Sure, yoga...could focus on Hindu or Buddhist gods...but it can also focus on Christ."[6] In fact, it is not a matter of "focus," but yoga was designed to create union with Hindu deities. It was never designed to "focus on Christ."

Paul and the apostles must have lived the epitome of Christianity in following Christ and bringing His gospel to the world of their day. There is not a hint that they ever practiced yoga. Nor does Hebrews 11, the "faith chapter," suggest that those who triumphed over every adversity—including martyrdom—practiced, needed, or had even heard of yoga. Far from having anything to do with the Christian life, much less with enhancing it, yoga could only be what Scripture calls "a way that seemeth right unto a man, but the end thereof are the ways of death" (Proverbs 14:12; 16:25).

Yoga and "Spirituality"

Mason's instructor at the hospital was Rebecca Laney. There is no denying the fact that yoga was developed in a culture that displays literally billions of images of the hundreds of millions of its gods. Every home in this yoga culture contains numerous depictions of the favorite gods the family members worship. Honestly reflecting this fact, Laney's Center for Yoga and Health in nearby Clinton "is decorated with a variety of Eastern and Western religious images, including small statues and pictures of Jesus, the Virgin Mary, the Buddha, and Hindu deities."[7]

It is blasphemy to associate pagan idols with the Lord Jesus Christ, who claimed to be the true God (and indeed is one with the Father). Clearly, to put Christ on the same level as "Buddha and Hindu deities" is not merely to mock Him but to deny Him altogether.

"Hindu deities" displayed in modern "Christian" America? The first two of the Ten Commandments declare: "Thou shalt have no other gods before me. Thou shalt not make unto thee any graven image...thou shalt not bow down thyself to them, nor serve them..." (Exodus 20:1-5). The Bible states repeatedly in so many ways that no willing heart could escape the truth: "I am God, and there is none else...there is no God else beside me.... Is there a God beside me...? I know not any" (Isaiah 44:6, 8; 45:5, 18, 21-22, etc.). As for other gods, whether "Hindu deities" or those of any other religion, the condemnation is clear:

> For all the gods of the nations are idols...the work of men's hands. They have mouths, but they speak not: eyes have they, but they see not: they have ears, but they hear not: noses have they, but they smell not: they have hands, but they handle not: feet have they, but they walk not: neither speak they through their throat. They that make them are like unto them; so is every one that trusteth in them." (Psalms 96:5; 115:4-8)

Turning her back on the Bible and ignoring the truth it so clearly and uncompromisingly declares, Laney claims that yoga "can enhance a person's spirituality—whatever it may be.... "[8] At least she is honestly admitting what many yoga instructors try to deny: there is a relationship between yoga and religion. But she could never honestly relate biblical Christianity to yoga.

We have noted the ecumenical claim that yoga fits all faiths— but it does not fit Christianity. In fact, it is the very antithesis of biblical Christianity. While the goal of yoga (following the Serpent's lie to Eve) is to enhance the self in the attempt to realize one's innate godhood, Christianity involves acknowledging that there is only one God, the Creator of all, and denying oneself to allow Christ, by His Spirit, to express Himself in one's life. As John the Baptist said, "He [Christ] must increase, but I must decrease" (John 3:30). Paul said, "In me...dwelleth no good thing" (Romans 7:18). It has been said: "If you want to be distracted, look around; if you want to be disgusted, look within; if you want to be delighted, look at Him."

Unbiblical "Spirituality"?

When Robin Norsted and Cindy Senarighi realized the spirituality in yoga, they decided to sell it in a package to others. They were especially impressed "by the spiritual aspect of the physical practice of yoga. As Christians, they experienced this as a devotional time in the presence of God." As a result, they founded Yogadevotion in 1999. They are convinced that Christians and non-Christians should be "using the physical practice of yoga to still their minds and be open to the relationship God intends for us." Their motto is, "Grow in faith and fitness through Yogadevotion classes."

For a private or semi-private session, the charge is $75 for one and a half hours. They also bring yoga to wedding showers, birthday parties and into churches to enhance "men's, women's, or children's ministry programs."[9] They teach Hatha Yoga and claim that it is purely physical—yet at the same time they claim to use it for "spiritual development." Their ads say, "Combining yoga poses with Christian music & thought-provoking devotions, Yogadevotion is a way to experience the presence of God through the physical expressions of yoga."[10]

Contrast this with the Bible's claim that God, through the

"exceeding great and precious promises" in His Word, has "given unto us all [not some] things that pertain unto life and godliness..." (2 Peter 1:3-11). Paul likewise declares that Scripture itself contains all that the Christian needs for "doctrine, for reproof, for correction, for instruction in righteousness: that the man [or woman, or boy, or girl] of God may be perfect [mature, complete], throughly furnished unto all good works" (2 Timothy 3:16-17). Clearly, to turn to yoga for "spirituality" (just as to turn to psychology for help) is to accuse the Bible of false promises and to charge the Holy Spirit with failing to include in His Word the instruction for all that the Christian needs for "life and godliness."

Nevertheless, "Christian yoga" continues its explosive growth in many churches and in yoga classes allegedly designed to enhance one's Christian faith. Susan Bordenkircher has turned this trend into a profitable business:

> [She] fell in love with yoga after attending a national yoga workshop. Susan is now a yoga instructor, certified in mind/body fitness through the Deep South Alliance.... She developed a unique class that combined the disciplines of yoga with her own Christian faith; the class is entitled Outstretched in Worship. Susan took a bold and novel approach by combining a routine of Hatha Yoga stretches and poses with Christian meditations.
>
> Due to the popularity of the class, Susan made the decision to develop a Christian yoga video series...in the Spring of 2002. The series is receiving a tremendous response nationally....[11]

Yoga as Religious Ritual

Clearly, the attempt to Christianize yoga raises other serious questions. What connection is there between "physical expressions of yoga," or any physical things, and God who, according to Jesus, "is a Spirit"? Actually, there is none except that we know He is the Creator of the physical universe. That does not mean, however, nor could it mean, that He is in or even connected to anything physical.

God created everything out of nothing, and the universe is separate and distinct from Him.[12] Nor could any physical object or action invented by man speak of or lead to God. Many objects (such as idols and fetishes) and many activities (such as pagan rituals and, yes, yoga) are designed to appease false gods. In that process, they lead one *away* from the true God. They could never lead us *to* Him.

Of course, certain physical objects or movements could arouse a deceptive emotion of "spirituality," but Jesus said, "God is a Spirit: and they that worship him must worship him in spirit and in truth" (John 4:24). Physical positions and movements cannot possibly in themselves convey spiritual truth. Much less can they be the means of accomplishing any spiritual good—and certainly not of putting man in touch with God. In fact, the use of physical objects or means in order to contact the spirit realm (and that includes God) are forbidden to the people of God and condemned as "divination" (Leviticus 19:31; 20:6; Deuteronomy 18:9-14, etc.). Furthermore, Paul warns that these physical objects formed by men for religious purposes are actually fronts for "devils": "the things which the Gentiles sacrifice, they sacrifice to devils, and not to God" (1 Corinthians 10:19-20).

Those who follow this path, no matter how well intentioned, are acting in direct disobedience to God's Word. At the mercy of their own subjective interpretations, they are soon led astray by their own hearts. Under the inspiration of the Holy Spirit, Jeremiah made this fact very clear:

> This evil people, which refuse to hear my words, which walk in the imagination of their heart, and walk after other gods, to serve them, and to worship them...the prophets prophesy lies in my name: I sent them not, neither have I commanded them, neither spake unto them: they prophesy unto you a false vision and divination...and the deceit of their heart. (Jeremiah 13:10; 14:14)

Yoga and Ecumenism

The film, *The Fire of Yoga*, also features massage therapist Julia Burr, who insists that "Yoga promotes spiritual growth because it feeds the body, mind, and soul. Drawing her own spirituality from Christianity and Zen Buddhism [totally incompatible], Burr, 59, said she particularly appreciates the meditative part of Yoga.... 'I wanted a deeper purpose to my life,' she said.... New York City-based filmmaker David Conway said he made the documentary because he wanted to tell the story of the transformative power of Yoga."[13] The promoters and practitioners of yoga seem unconcerned that so often the "transformative power of yoga" proves to be destructive. That fact will be documented in later chapters.

Many Christians in the Western world, concerned by the fact that yoga is "an Eastern religion," are rightfully fearful that practicing yoga "might undermine their own religious faith." Of the tens of thousands of websites dealing with "Christian Yoga," however, most promise that instead of undermining one's personal faith in Christ, "yoga can actually deepen it." Many of these websites honestly acknowledge that "yoga has historically been associated with India's three great religious-cultural traditions—Hinduism, Buddhism, and Jainism"—and that its teachings "are infused with many concepts that have a Hindu, Buddhist, or Jaina flavor." Yet the claim is made that the "deities (deva) of Hinduism, Buddhism, and Jainism can be compared to the angels of Christianity and Judaism." As we have seen, however, the Apostle Paul, under the inspiration of the Holy Spirit, called them "devils."[14]

In a further whitewash, assurance is given that specific "beliefs are not essential to Yoga practice...we need not believe in anything other than the possibility that we can transform ourselves [because] we have not yet tapped into our full potential." It is yoga that allegedly will "put us in touch with our spiritual core—our innermost nature—that which or who we truly are."[15] Again, this purpose of yoga is diametrically opposed to the clear teaching of Christ and the entire Bible. So how can so many Christians claim that it benefits their relationship to God? Could they be falling for a dangerous deception?

Though finding their "spiritual core" may not be why most Americans are attracted at first to yoga, they are soon swept in that direction without realizing it. Almost inevitably, they sooner or later come to accept this new emphasis as an unexpected and beneficial bonus. By that time, they have been drawn in so deeply that it will be almost impossible to turn back from the downward path—a path they never intended to take when they first got involved in yoga "for the physical benefits."

The ecumenical ignorance surrounding yoga seemingly knows no bounds. A typical message on a chat line declares:

Jesus Christ himself taught a form of yoga. But usually "christians" just don't get it. I'm a christian myself and practice yoga the way Jesus taught it...it's sad that usually my fellow christians don't understand this stuff and I'm accused of blasphemy. When you mention yoga and Jesus in the same sentence you're going to get quite a lecture.[16]

Jesus "taught yoga"? This person may have something that he calls "the Bible," but he can't have a true Bible, because *anything* about yoga, much less about Jesus *teaching* yoga, is missing entirely from God's true Word.

Obviously, the writer knows nothing about the God of the Bible and mankind's rebellion against this God, or about the judgment God has pronounced upon sin because of His holiness, or that the eternal Son of God came to earth, became a man through a virgin birth, died in payment of the full penalty for our sins, rose from the dead, and that it is only through faith in Him that we can be forgiven. There are many who dishonestly call themselves Christians. Why "dishonestly"? It is not honest to call oneself a follower of Christ while ignoring and even rejecting His teachings and example.

Serious Questions

Are Jesus and yoga in any way compatible? If not, why not—and what could the consequences be? What is the truth, and which side should we be on in this growing controversy? We want to consider these important questions in the following pages. We cannot ignore the fact that Americans continue to embrace yoga at an astonishing rate. Why are they doing so? According to a survey taken by YogaJournal.com:

1. Most yoga practitioners said they did yoga for health and physical benefits....

2. Thirty percent of the 1,555 yoga practitioners who participated in the web survey indicated that the goal of their yoga practice was to stay fit and toned.

3. Others practiced to reduce stress (21 percent), to remedy a health problem (18 percent), [to] pursue the path to enlightenment (16 percent) and to engage in spiritual practice (15 percent).[17]

In addition to liberal churches, yoga is accepted in many schools, city recreation programs, YMCAs, YWCAs, and adult-education classes, to name a few of the sponsoring organizations. At the same time, many "church people" still distrust yoga, most often because of an unsettling feeling that perhaps they are involving themselves in something not-quite Christian but very much "New Age." This uneasiness persists for many despite solemn protests to the contrary from most yoga instructors and practitioners—and from many Christian leaders as well.

Such was the very concern of Dr. Scott Morris. Both a physician and an ordained Methodist minister, he was drawn into the practice of yoga and became convinced of its benefits. With some trepidation, Dr. Morris began offering yoga classes at the Hope and Healing Center in Memphis, Tennessee, more than two years before this present book went to press. The venture was a great success, if popularity is any indication. Indeed, that seems to be a sufficient basis of acceptance for most of those who become involved. Here is Morris's own account of what happened:

> "A lot of what we do here may be perceived as on the edge of what might be acceptable," said Morris. "It was important for me to be convinced. It was important for me that it had

support from the medical point of view and that we got the right people to teach it."

Then he worried whether people would come to the classes. They did. The first classes filled up within five minutes, he said. Now he's a believer.[18]

Does popularity define holiness and obedience? Is truth determined by vote? Sadly, that seems to be the basis of faith and practice for many Christians. This is especially true for members of those churches that adjust Christianity and the gospel to the tastes of the ungodly in order to promote "church growth."

The Swiss psychiatrist, C. G. Jung, was intimately acquainted with yoga (including Kundalini yoga, which we will deal with later) and most forms of Eastern mysticism. The son of a Protestant minister, Jung was raised in the Swiss state church, which was totally apostate then, as it remains today. His father was a spirit medium and a Mason. Jung's doctoral dissertation was about spiritism, which he practiced throughout his life. He was well acquainted with all forms of Eastern mysticism.

Jung was certainly not a true Christian in the biblical sense of the word. Nevertheless, he pulled the rug out from under "Christian yoga" long before anyone had invented that incredible idea. Jung declared, "But you cannot be a good Christian, either in your faith or in your morality or in your intellectual make-up, and practice genuine yoga at the same time. I have seen too many cases...."[19]

Chanting "OM"

Very much a part of yoga is the chanting of "Om," a breathing sound that instructors often ask their students to use to quiet them down, focus their energies, and help "get themselves centered." Yet they are seldom told that "Om" (pronounced "Aauum") is believed by the yogis in the East to be the basic sound of the universe underlying all "Being" and that chanting it is designed to unite one with the "universal deity"! This purpose is seldom explained in the West. Why the deliberate cover-up? Yoga continues to be promoted by false advertising—and Congress not only grants it credibility but endorses it!

Yogis in the East teach that chanting "Om" is a form of surrender to the basic force pervading the universe—but what does that really mean? Laurette Willis, who was led into New Age occultism through yoga and was then delivered through faith in Christ and obedience to God's Word explains: "The goal of all yoga is to obtain oneness with the universe. That's also known as the process of enlightenment, or union with Brahman (Hinduism's highest god). The word 'yoga' means 'union,' or 'to yoke'.... Yoga wants to get students to the point of complete numbness in their minds [to open them to this force]. God, on the other hand, wants you to be transformed by the renewing of your mind through his Word."[20]

In contrast to the relaxation exercises of yoga, which are specifically designed to empty the mind, the desire of the true God, Creator of the universe, is to bring us into a willing, understanding, and conscious relationship with Himself—a relationship based not upon mystical states of mind but upon truth and love. Speaking through His prophet Jeremiah, God declared: "But let him that glorieth glory in this, that he understandeth and knoweth me, that

I am the LORD which exercise lovingkindness, judgment, and righteousness, in the earth: for in these things I delight..." (Jeremiah 9:24). Notice that "understanding" is placed first and is the foundation of "knowing."

Satan offers many counterfeits, which are easily recognized because they all deny God's truth. Jesus Christ solemnly declared: "I am the way, the truth, and the life: no man cometh unto the Father, but by me" (John 14:6). In love, He warned: "Enter ye in at the strait gate: for wide is the gate, and broad is the way, that leadeth to destruction, and many there be which go in thereat: Because strait is the gate, and narrow is the way, which leadeth unto life, and few there be that find it" (Matthew 7:13-14). "Christian yoga" promises assistance along the broader path that God said leads not to health and well-being but rather to destruction.

"The purpose of chanting is only to soften the palate and to open the channels to the body," said one instructor, although she didn't indicate how this "opening up" process was expected to take place, nor why her students would need to "soften their palates" when, presumably, they were not involved in voice lessons. "Open the channels to the body" for what? Obviously not for food or drink, so it must mean for something nonphysical—something "spiritual." Beware!

"A lot of times people won't come to Yoga because they feel fearful," she added. But "Yoga is not the Antichrist. It's movement with breath and precision. It's a way for people to pursue their own spiritual beliefs. It deepens your connection to what you believe in."[21] So, once again, we have the admission that yoga is "spiritual," along with the usual denial that this should be of any concern because it fits with anyone's spirituality or religion, take your pick.

Of course, this entire idea of a physical-spiritual interchange is a delusion. In fact, this is the very lie with which Satan deceived Eve in the Garden: the belief that something physical (the fruit of the Tree of the Knowledge of Good and Evil) could infuse her with spiritual life and turn her into a god. This story is true history, and it alone explains man's rebellion against God and the evil that followed and grows worse each day. Yet Jung, an unbeliever who has led millions astray, called Eden a "therapeutic myth."

Many fantastic claims are made for yoga: that its physical positions, movements, and breathing exercises form a bridge not only to spirituality in general but to the specific religion of each person. It is too much to believe! Yet this ancient lie in many other forms continues to deceive. In the following pages, we will examine this claim and discover what this "spiritual power" is to which yoga opens those who practice it.

How Many Ways through Yoga to "God"?

If we are to understand yoga, we need to go back to its beginnings. Those who first began the practice believed there were an infinite number of ways to "god," or "the Divine" within. Theoretically, any religion would do. But yoga, they concluded, through the altered state of consciousness that it was designed to create, was the best path, and it was divided into four major categories: Jnana-yoga, Bhakti-yoga, Karma-yoga, and Raja-yoga. The ultimate goal of each is the same: self-realization, culminating in union with the ALL, of which the universe and all within it are but myriad expressions.

Jnana-yoga is detailed in the Hindu *Upanisads*, which are the distillation of the insights of numerous "self-realized masters" presenting "Vedantic truths" over a period of some 1,000 years or more. Bhakti-yoga involves devotion to the gods and goddesses, such as Vishnu, Rama, Kali, or Krishna, in order to merge into "the Divine." Karma-yoga involves right actions offered to the Divine in payment for past misdeeds, as expounded particularly in the *Bhagavad-Gita* by Sri Krishna to the warrior Arjuna. Raja-yoga is the royal path and considered by many to be the most powerful and effective way to union with the Divine. It involves special techniques for altering consciousness in order to encounter the Divine, as set forth largely in Patanjali's *Yoga Sutras.*

Clearly, whatever physical conditioning is involved in any form of yoga, it is but a means to the spiritual objective that all forms have in common. If that fact doesn't cause warning bells to sound in one's head and heart, then nothing will! As we say a number of times throughout this book, if one is interested in physical fitness, then by all means adopt exercises specifically designed to that end.

In contrast, yoga, though parts of it may be physically beneficial, was designed—through its physical positions, stretching, and breathing exercises—to yoke practitioners with the Divine allegedly within us all. One cannot adopt even the physical aspects of yoga without becoming spiritually ensnared. This is a fact rooted in history, which no amount of denial by Western yoga instructors can change.

It is true that the yogic *asanas* (physical positions) can have a dramatic effect upon the body and may even lead to improved health. Likewise, the *pranayama* (regulation of breathing) may seem to do the same. The ultimate goal of all yoga, however, as Jung clearly understood, remains the awakening, through the asanas and pranayama, the Kundalini "divine power," portrayed as a serpent coiled three and a half times when at rest at the base of the spine. Awakened, it moves up through the seven *chakras* along the spine and bursts into the "thousand-petalled lotus" in the cerebral cortex.

At that point, the yogi is flooded with the divine ecstasy of the alleged union of *atman* (the individual self) with *Brahman* (the universal self), resulting in the self-realization of "that thou art." This could involve tantra, with uncontrollable sexual urges, and other dangers. Thus the ancient texts warn the novice yogi coming into self-realization always to have his guru present for protection from potential disaster. Such is the clear caveat repeated by all of the ancient founders of authentic yoga. Tragically, this fact is either not known to, or is deliberately ignored by, most yoga instructors in the West today.

An Appeal to Investigate and Face All the Facts

It can all sound so good, however, in the enticing language of the yogis. For example, Sri Swami Sivananda, one of the most highly respected gurus to come from India to the West for the express purpose of enlightening Americans, promises that the self-realization produced by yoga will bring supreme and eternal happiness:

> All agree that the one aim which man has in all his acts is to secure happiness for himself. The highest as well as the ultimate end of man must, therefore, be to attain eternal, infinite, unbroken, supreme happiness. This happiness can be had in one's own Self or Atman only. Therefore, search within to attain this eternal Bliss.[22]

Such instruction isn't even rational—and certainly contradicts the Bible. If "eternal bliss" is already "within" and can only "be had in one's Self or Atman," why must one search for it? It sounds like the delusion that led astray a generation of hippies and was expressed in their pitiful plea: "I'm just trying to find myself."

As for the Self, Jesus said, "For out of the heart proceed evil thoughts, murders, adulteries, fornications, thefts, false witness, blasphemies... (Matthew 15:19). Paul confessed, "For I know that in me (that is, in my flesh,) dwelleth no good thing: for to will is present with me; but how to perform that which is good I find not" (Romans 7:18-25). The Bible provides true wisdom: "Seek ye the LORD [not self] while he may be found, call ye upon him while he is near..." (Isaiah 55:6).

Rabi Maharaj, at one time a yogi and Hindu guru, was delivered by Christ from the "gods" he faithfully served but who eventually tried to destroy him. He advises, "If you want to enhance your health, adopt an exercise program specifically designed to do just that. Don't get involved in exercises that were designed and practiced for thousands of years as a means of 'self-realization,' i.e., realizing that you are 'god,' one with the universe."

With so many opinions, what is the real truth about yoga—or is there one? How can it be spiritually beneficial if one only adopts the physical aspects of yoga? The answer to such questions becomes ever more urgent as this practice spreads. What about yoga? How can contradictory views diametrically opposed to one another all be valid? Does it matter? *Christianity Today* won't take a position in this growing controversy but publishes opinions on both sides. To take that neutral position is not helpful in resolving the important issues involved.

The great importance of this subject demands that we know the truth, and knowing the truth always requires choosing sides. Since beliefs that contradict one another on the very fundamentals cannot all be true, the truth must oppose and be opposed by what is false. What is true "spirituality" and what is false? That is the most important issue anyone could face—and that is the question we will pursue with great care in the following pages.

1. http://www.local6.com/news/5313050/detail.html.

2. Jacinthia Jones, "Yoga, religion work hand in hand," *Naples (Florida) Daily News,* August 23, 2003.

3. *The Kansas City Star*, Religion Notes, April 9, 2005.

4. Jean Gordon, "Faith, healing and...yoga," *The Clarion-Ledger*, February 12, 2005.

5. http://www.ysmarko.com/?p=232.

6. Ibid.

7. http://www.clarionledger.com/apps/pbcs.dll/article?AID=/20050212/FEAT05/502120318/1023.

8. Gordon, "Faith."

9. http://www.yogadevotion.com.

10. http://www.firstlutheranwbl.org/ministries/yogaDevotion.htm.

11. http://www.christianyoga.us/instructor.htm.

12. Hebrews 11:3.

13. Gordon, "Faith."

14. 1 Corinthians 10:20.

15. http://shambhala.com/html/learn/features/yoga/basics/religion.cfm.

16. http://www.yoga.com/forums/forums/thread-view.asp?tid=18143&start=16&posts=24.

17. http://www.yogajournal.com/meditation/750_1.cfm.

18. Jones, "Yoga."

19. C. G. Jung, *Collected Works of C. G. Jung*, Sir Herbert Read, Michael Fordham, Gerhard Adler, William McGuire, eds. (Princeton NJ: Princeton University Press, 1969), 500.

20. Holly Vincente Robaina, *The Truth About Yoga*, www.christianitytoday.com/tcw/2005/002/14.40.html.

21. Jones, "Yoga."

22. Sri Swami Sivananda, *Kundalini Yoga* (Uttar Pradesh, India: Divine Life Society Publication, 1999), Preface.

—3—

THE AQUARIAN CONSPIRACY

"Yoga is undergoing something of a boom in Japan.... New yoga studios are popping up all over the capital and it's no longer rare to see women carrying their mats as they scamper around the streets of trendier Tokyo districts.... Japanese now into yoga have created such incredible demand that there [are] not enough teachers to sate their needs."[1]

Yet Ken Harakuma, who operates the IYC yoga studio in the Tokyo suburb of Ogikubo and claims to have been the first yoga instructor to operate in Japan, is not happy. He claims that "Many instructors...want nothing more than their students to be able to strike up a few poses.... What is supposed to happen is that when you take up a particular position, it teaches you how to create energy and how that energy can be used...[otherwise] it has no right to call itself yoga." He continues:

Students are creating energy but don't know how to use it, so the energy ends up being used the wrong way. This can lead to physical and mental harm....[2]

Harakuma is one of the very few yoga instructors today who acknowledge its dangers and seek to warn the unwary. Yoga creates "energy" that could do physical and mental harm? Obviously he isn't speaking only of physical energy, though many practitioners would claim that's all there is to it. The true yogis from India, however, refer to yoga as the means of arousing a spiritual energy that they believe generates amazing psychic powers that could be very destructive.

There is mounting controversy among Westerners involved in yoga as to how to practice it and the purpose behind it. Is it purely physical or is something more involved—something spiritual? There are many proponents on both sides of this discussion. Most of the public, however, are not even aware of the issue. Nor can most of the disputants even agree to what is meant by "spiritual." Clearly something nonphysical is involved. But what is it?

What is this "energy" to which Ken Harakuma (and others) are referring? Is this the ki, or chi, of martial arts, which has no physical explanation and clearly comes from the spirit world? Yet in spite of warnings backed with factual data about its dangers—and that it can even open the door to the occult—yoga continues to grow in popularity everywhere. What is behind the accelerating worldwide interest in yoga?

The Surprising Roots of New Age "Spirituality"

We are the most highly informed and sophisticated society in history and are currently in the midst of a hi-tech explosion beyond anyone's wildest imagination only a few years ago. Yet at the same time, increasing millions in the West are buying into yoga, an occult practice that has been part of primitive Oriental superstitions and religions for thousands of years. Why is this happening? Finding an answer to that question will give us a good start toward understanding what yoga really is, why it is so appealing, and the havoc it is wreaking upon our culture.

Though it may come as a surprise, the fact is that the explosion of occultism in the West (of which yoga is an integral part) did not come about by accident. This growing obsession was deliberately planted and cultivated by a group of psychologists and physical scientists, many of whom had, as university students, their first encounters with the mysterious powers of the occult and came to believe in the reality of a nonphysical dimension through their use of psychedelic drugs. The major drug of what became known as the "counter-culture" was lysergic acid diethylamide (LSD), a once legal but now illegal substance commonly called "acid" by its users. It was developed in 1943 by Albert Hoffman, a chemist at the Swiss pharmaceutical company, Sandoz A. B.

"Consciousness" became a primary focus, and soon the phrase "alternate states of consciousness" was on the lips of millions. How to reach "alternate states" became the exciting topic at parties and was the new panacea. Few even suspected that they had stumbled onto the doorway to the occult, much less the horrors that lay beyond.

Of course, the world of academia, closed-minded to anything except materialistic explanations, spoke of an "alternate reality" as though it were a newly discovered unused corner of the physical brain that held amazing potential and must be studied in university labs. The "Human Potential Movement" was born. Mankind's supposedly unlimited and untapped powers became the new hope of the modern world, bolstered by the psychologists' ridiculous claim that we use only 10 percent of our brains. In that unused 90 percent, god-like psychic powers supposedly lie, awaiting discovery.

"Ironically," wrote Marilyn Ferguson, in a key book of this era, "the introduction of major psychedelics like LSD in the 1960s was largely attributable to the Central Intelligence Agency's investigation into these drugs for possible military use. Experiments on more than eighty college campuses, under various CIA code names, unintentionally popularized LSD. Thousands of graduate students served as guinea pigs. Soon they were synthesizing their own 'acid.'"[3]

Unintentionally? On the contrary, this devilish development was anything but *unintentional,* as Ferguson well knew. It was, as we shall see, part of a deliberate and highly secretive plan to initiate the Western world into Eastern occultism, of which the introduction of drugs to American youth played a major part. Under the influence of psychedelics, millions discovered another dimension of reality that surely was not physical. But as long as the "trip" lasted, the adventure was as real as the physical universe—or, seemingly, even more real.

It only remained to be discovered that yoga would produce the same "trip" without drugs—and yoga took off as the new panacea. I remember the mother of a 20-year-old telling me with some sense of relief and little concern, "Our son used to be heavily into drugs; but thank God he isn't using drugs anymore because he started practicing yoga. I don't know what yoga is, but it can't be bad if it got him off of drugs!"

My reply must have shocked her: "I'm glad to hear that your son no longer gets 'high' on drugs. I'm sorry to inform you, however, that he can get a lot 'higher' on yoga than on drugs. Drugs were the kindergarten of occultism—yoga is the graduate school!"

A Devilish Development?

Sir John Eccles, Nobel Prize winner for his research on the brain, described it as "a machine that a ghost can operate." Famed neurologist Wilder Penfield declared: "The brain is a computer...programmed by something outside itself, the mind."[4] Normally, one's own spirit (mind) uses the "brain-computer" to connect with the body and the space-time-matter continuum in which our bodies function. In an "altered state," whether reached through certain drugs, under hypnosis, or induced by yoga (wittingly or unwittingly), the normal connection between spirit and brain is loosened. That disconnection allows another spirit entity to interpose itself and operate the brain, creating a universe of illusion, including the alleged "self-realization" of being a god in complete unity with the universe. This same promise was made to Eve by the Serpent if she would only disobey the true God and follow the Serpent's seductive directions.

The scientific description of what happens to the brain in an "altered state" could very well explain not merely drug-related delusions but how humans become vulnerable (or deliberately open themselves) to what is commonly known as "demonic possession." In fact, yoga was designed to do precisely that—but it was called "spirit possession," and the "spirits" were presumed to be Hindu deities, some benevolent, some destructive. Yoga is to Hindus what peyote is to native Americans in their religion: a doorway into the spirit world and contact with entities that may become one's guide, guardian—or destroyer. As already noted, the ancient yogis warned of the dangers that yoga posed to practitioners, declaring that one's guru must always be present during the "awakening" that yoga was designed to produce.

Only pride and blindness of Himalayan proportions could cause us humans to imagine that we are the only minds in the universe! That admission came reluctantly on the part of many scientists, and especially psychologists, whose pseudo-science treats man as merely a conglomeration of interrelated molecules wired by nerves—a physical stimulus-response mechanism with sophisticated feedback. But that theory cannot explain the desire for purpose and meaning or the universal recognition of right, wrong, justice, and injustice. These concepts have no relationship to the physical universe of time and sense but exist only in the mind. Materialism died with the recognition that the mind is not physical.

The Evolution Delusion

Evolutionists attempted to salvage a semi-materialism by proposing that souls and spirits "evolved" from bodies. Robert Jastrow (founder and for many years director of the Goddard Institute for Space Studies) theorized that had evolution been going on for billions of years longer on some other planets than on Earth it might have produced nonphysical entities now inhabiting our universe in disembodied form. Being nonphysical—and thus free from the limitations of space, matter, and time—they could theoretically have instant access to any part of the material universe.

The utterly hopeless mathematical odds against the molecules comprising the tiniest cell ever coming together into the proper order by chance prove that evolution is impossible. Period! It couldn't even get *started* at the molecular level. End of discussion. For example, Sir Fred Hoyle, world-renowned astronomer and one of the most creative scientists of the twentieth century, calculated that the odds of producing by chance only the enzymes necessary for life were one in ten with 40,000 zeros added. He claimed that "everyone knows it's impossible," yet it continues to be taught because supporting the theory is essential to maintaining one's academic standing.

Nevertheless, Jastrow's hypothesis is interesting for other reasons:

> Life that is a billion years beyond us may be far beyond the flesh-and-blood form that we would recognize. It may [have] escaped its mortal flesh to become something that old-fashioned people would call spirits.
>
> And so how do we know it's there? Maybe it can materialize and then dematerialize. I'm sure it has magical powers by our standards....[5]

Imagine scientists attempting communication with ("highly evolved") nonphysical entities! Physical science has no means of either identifying these entities or verifying the truthfulness of their intentions or what they say. If demons (Satan's minions) actually exist, as the Bible declares, they themselves couldn't have invented a more seductive lie to opening the door for contacting and deceiving mankind.

Clearly, the only means of contact would be through "spirit mediums" who claim the ability to communicate with such entities. What a set-up for Satan! In fact, as we have documented elsewhere,[6] the messages that come allegedly from the spirit world, whether through mediums, channelers, during yogic trance, "mental telepathy," under hypnosis, or other similar means, consistently communicate the same lies with which the Serpent deceived Eve in the Garden of Eden. This can hardly be a coincidence!

Evolution's "Gods" for Modern Man

Jastrow, who did not believe in the true God, Creator of the universe, hypothesizes creatures produced by evolution that have the characteristics of gods! Presumably, we could look to them for salvation—if we could make contact and if they were benevolent and had any interest in saving us. But saving us from what? And why would they even care if we existed? Apart from the incorruptible God, who has proven His goodness, power corrupts, so if they are the most powerful creatures in existence, they would likely be the most selfish. All of this speculation is beside the point, however, because such creatures don't exist and we didn't evolve—we were created and are responsible to our Creator.

For the materialist, evolution is the only explanation for existence. But that explains nothing. It is absurd to speculate about matter evolving into living forms when science cannot explain the origin of the energy of which matter and living cells are composed!

The first law of thermodynamics, the law of the conservation of energy, declares that energy can neither be created nor destroyed. It must therefore have existed forever—but that conclusion is contradicted by the second law, the law of entropy, which declares that energy entropies (i.e., becomes less and less usable). If energy had been here forever, it should already have run itself down like a clock (entropied completely) eons ago—yet this is clearly not the case.

Unquestionably, the universe and the energy of which every

physical thing is composed had a beginning—a fact admitted by Jastrow himself. It could only have been created, and out of nothing, within the finite past by an eternal and all-powerful Being who is without beginning or end. That conclusion is inescapable. The only reason for attempting to deny this fact is the desire to escape accountability to the Creator. But hiding one's head in the sand of denial will not change the facts.

The first words in the Bible are: "In the beginning God created the heaven and the earth" (Genesis 1:1). The Bible certainly got that right—reason enough to give the Bible an open-minded hearing. This ancient book was written by about 40 different men over a period of some 1,600 years. Most of them came from different cultures and times in history and never knew one another. The only common factor for most of these men was their claim to inspiration from the one true God, Creator of all—and their supernatural writings can be explained on no other basis.

The wisdom in the Bible was not drawn from but is far beyond the science and philosophy of the times and cultures in which the prophets who wrote it lived. Its hundreds of prophecies foretold the future centuries and even thousands of years in advance, and history records their *unfailing accuracy.* The Bible's major themes run from beginning to end without any contradictions, either internally or from true science.

The Role Being Played by Nonphysical Beings

The Bible declares that we are not alone in the universe but that in addition to mankind, there are angels, demons, Satan, and God—all with individual minds that think and make decisions for themselves. Parapsychologists (especially those associated with the Department of Defense and government Intelligence agencies) have been involved for years in mind-control research. Some of it has nothing to do with controlling minds through drugs or brainwashing techniques but with control of one person's mind by another person's mind. This possibility, of course, has been demonstrated repeatedly through hypnosis—even at a distance.

There is, therefore, good reason to believe that, just as a hypnotist can control someone else's mind, so the other minds mentioned above could do the same to humans. God would never do this Himself because it would nullify the freedom of choice He has given to mankind in the act of creation. It is also both logical and biblical that He would build protection within man to prevent a take-over of the human mind by any other mind. One could, however, voluntarily allow this to be done by willingly submitting to hypnosis. Moreover, deliberately entering an altered state, whether through drugs, hypnosis, or yoga, is giving permission to evil entities to take over, whether one realizes it or not.

Charles Tart, author of *Mind Science: Meditation Training for Practical People*, says, "There's enough evidence that comes in to make me take the idea of disembodied intelligence seriously."[7] William James, one of the most highly regarded psychologists of the last century, wrote: "The refusal of modern 'enlightenment' to treat '[demonic] possession' as a hypothesis...has always seemed to me a curious example of the power of fashion in things 'scientific.'"[8]

Anthropologist Michael Harner wrote, "A shaman...enters an altered state of consciousness...to acquire...special, personal power, which is usually supplied by his guardian and helping spirits."[9] John Lilly, who invented the isolation tank (in which one floats in a sea of heavy salt water, completely isolated from sights or sounds of the world) that inspired the movie, *Altered States*, declared: "Some people call it 'lucid dreaming.' It's a lot easier if you have a psychedelic in you, but a lot of people...can just meditate and go into these alternate realities...."[10] There are many recorded accounts by those who have experienced similar adventures and "possession" while practicing yoga.

Marilyn Ferguson Called it a "Conspiracy"

In 1974, a think tank at Stanford Research Institute (known as SRI), with funds from the Charles F. Kettering Foundation, completed a study called *Changing Images of Man*. Reading this important unpublished study, one arrives at the following startling conclusion concerning its purpose: to determine how Western man could deliberately be turned into an Eastern mystic/psychic. The project was directed by Willis W. Harman, who later became president of Edgar Mitchell's Institute of Noetic Sciences, founded by Mitchell as a result of mystical experiences on his trip to the moon. The scientists involved sincerely believed that turning to Eastern mysticism was the only hope for human survival.[11] In their own minds, their reasons were all very scientific and their intentions noble. The end, it was believed, justified the means.

The 319-page mimeographed report was prepared by a team of fourteen researchers and supervised by a panel of twenty-three controllers, including anthropologist Margaret Mead, psychologist B. F. Skinner, Ervin Laszlo of the United Nations, and Sir Geoffrey Vickers of British intelligence. The task of persuading the public to walk through this magic door leading to a "new age" fell to one of Dr. Harman's friends and admirers, Marilyn Ferguson. She fulfilled her assignment with the publication in 1980 of her groundbreaking bestseller, *The Aquarian Conspiracy*, which made it all seem very desirable. She wrote:

A great, shuddering irrevocable shift is overtaking us...a new mind, a turnabout in consciousness in critical numbers of individuals, a network powerful enough to bring about radical change in our culture.

This network—the Aquarian Conspiracy—has already enlisted the minds, hearts and resources of some of our most advanced thinkers, including Nobel laureate scientists, philosophers, statesmen, celebrities...who are working to create a different kind of society.... There are legions of [Aquarian] conspirators. They are in corporations, universities, and hospitals, on the faculties of public schools, in factories and doctors' offices, in state and federal agencies, on city councils, and the White House staff, in state legislatures, in volunteer organizations, in virtually all arenas of policy making in the country.

The [Eastern mystical] technologies for expanding and transforming personal consciousness, once the secret of an elite, are now generating massive change in every cultural institution—medicine, politics, business, education, religion, and the family.[12]

A major reason for changing the "image of man" had apparently already been demonstrated through successful experiments at SRI in "Remote Viewing" (RV). We cannot go into the details,[13] but suffice it to say that under strict laboratory (and even military intelligence) tests, certain persons proved to have a demonstrable ability to describe places, persons, and events anywhere in the universe and in the past, present, or future.[14] The three best known Remote Viewers were Ingo Swann, Pat Price, and Hella Hammid. Their abilities have been demonstrated in everything from spying on foreign military targets to finding lost wrecks, whether of planes recently downed or ancient ships.

Swann has a great deal to say about yoga, which he considers to be a way to develop paranormal powers of the mind. In fact, he has given careful attention to a study of ancient yoga texts, which he found to be "a treasure trove of additional information" related to RV abilities.[15]

Another author states, "Yoga, an ancient Indian technique for achieving altered states of consciousness, is said to awaken in the individual abilities which sound very much like those of the shaman and magician.... The *Yoga Sutras* of Patanjali, compiled around the 3rd century BCE, speak of such abilities—in fact, the third part of the book is entirely devoted to the various 'powers' that are apparently acquired during the practice of Yoga."[16] Many have found that these "psychic abilities" suddenly appeared uninvited as a result of practicing what they thought had been purely physical yoga—and with unwelcome and devastating spiritual results.

The Drug Connection and its Gurus

Among the many key events (too many to be included here) in turning our youth to drugs and the East (which opened the door to yoga) was the publication in 1954 of Aldous Huxley's book, *The Doors of Perception*. In 1953, Huxley had been given a large supply of mescaline for his personal use by Dr. Humphrey Osmond, his private physician. What he experienced in the altered states of consciousness under that drug convinced him of its value as a psychological tool. *The Doors of Perception* became the first manifesto of the psychedelic drug cult. Its claim that hallucinogenic drugs "expand consciousness" was ideally suited to the mindset of the hippies and justified the "mind trips" that they came to believe would accelerate their "liberation" from society.

Huxley helped found the Esalen Institute in Big Sur, California, which became a mecca for New Agers of all stripes for experimentation in psychic powers and spirit communication. Hundreds of

Americans came there to engage in weekends of T-Groups (using biofeedback, role-playing, etc., to gain insights into themselves, others, and groups, in order to change the standards, attitudes, and behavior of individuals) and Training Groups, modeled on behavior group therapy, to practice Zen, Hindu, and Buddhist transcendental meditation, and "out of body" experiences through simulated and actual hallucinogenic drugs ingestion.[17]

Timothy Leary, Harvard psychology professor (until he was dismissed in 1963), was privately purchasing large quantities of LSD from Sandoz pharmaceutical for his own personal use and for distribution.[18] He became the pied piper of the drug era, which paved the way for Eastern mysticism, including yoga, to invade the West. His admirers honored him as "the Galileo of Consciousness." A belligerent atheist, one of his sayings was "beware of monotheism." Leary opposed the family and moral absolutes, considered LSD and what it did to the nervous system to be a natural and essential part of the next stage in human evolution, and tried to establish psilocybin as treatment for reforming criminals.

Leary's book, *The Psychedelic Experience,* based on the ancient Buddhist *Tibetan Book of the Dead* (which C. G. Jung regarded so highly that he carried a copy with him everywhere), became another "bible" of the counter-culture, and millions followed his advice. As one commentary on that book declares:

> More often than not the dazzling and multi-colored archetypes that sprang forth came in the exotic guise of the gods and demons of India and Tibet. Mystical experience and the spiritual quest became synonymous with drug-induced altered states of consciousness and the search for the ultimate "high." The message of the day: "tune in, turn on, drop out." Following a commonly held belief that many of Asia's revered scriptures could be utilized most effectively

in the west by replacing their sacred images with western ones, former Harvard psychology professors Timothy Leary and Richard Alpert (aka Ram Dass), enthusiasts of the new counter-culture, took the *Tibetan Book of the Dead* and presented it as a guidebook for the LSD experience.[19]

Under the influence of psychedelic drugs, America's hippies, followed Timothy Leary's advice to "Tune in, turn on, and drop out." In doing so, they experienced a nonphysical dimension of existence that seemed to be at least as real as normal consciousness. Thus, multitudes of America's youth began in earnest the purposeful pursuit of "altered states of consciousness" in the attempt to finally "find themselves." Godlike powers were allegedly available within, awaiting discovery. These were the treasure of "infinite potential" promised by the Human Potential Movement, also known as the New Age Movement. Many following this trail found that it eventually led them to yoga.

"Spiritual but Not Religious"

The use of mind-altering drugs was touted as the short-cut to "spirituality," vital to the quest for "freedom," and was looked upon as sure evidence of personal growth. The saying (still heard today), "I'm spiritual but not religious," became the justification for one's own "experience" (whether on drugs or not) to be the sole determinant of truth. From that attitude, other slogans were spawned, such as, "Whatever works for you is okay," or "You've got your god, I've got mine," or "Well, that's your truth, but not mine," etc. As in Hinduism, everything was *maya* (an illusion), and it was up to each individual to create his own "reality" in his imagination. Truth ceased to be objective, absolutes were rejected, and, as became the case in early Israel, everyone did "that which was right in his own eyes" (Judges 17:6).

Entranced by the new universe of the mind, which they discovered in the "altered states of consciousness" created by LSD and other psychedelics, multitudes were hooked on the "spiritual experiences" they had on drug trips. To those who were educated to believe in a purely material universe, it was a shock to gain access to a nonphysical universe that was every bit as real as the material one. Mind-altering substances opened the door to new adventures, not the least exciting of which was meeting "spirit guides." The fact that psychiatrists began to prescribe LSD for personality treatment, and a hallucinogenic drug experimental clinic was established at Palo Alto Veterans Administration Hospital, are only two of the amazing developments of this period.

Beginning in 1962, the Rand Corporation of Santa Monica, California, began a four-year experiment in LSD, peyote, and marijuana. In 1963, the Beatles arrived in the United States. After their triumphant introduction on the Ed Sullivan Show, the "British sound" took America by storm. But the source of their inspiration was unquestionably demonic. All of the rock groups were on drugs, and their fans followed suit. Drugs and rock music simply go together—and most lyrics and scores were written under the influence of "spirit entities" contacted in altered states induced by LSD or other hallucinogens. Of his songwriting, John Lennon said, "It's like being possessed: like a psychic or a medium."[20] He told of mystical experiences as a teenager: "I used to literally trance out into alpha...seeing these hallucinatory images of my face changing, becoming cosmic and complete."[21]

Radio stations in San Francisco and New York City were

among the first to push the "Liverpool Sound"—the hard rock of the Rolling Stones, the Beatles, and the Animals. They would later pioneer "acid rock" and, eventually, psychotic "punk rock." The Beatles' press agent, Derek Taylor, in a now well-known interview, confessed: "They're completely anti-Christ. I mean, I am anti-Christ as well, but they're so anti-Christ they shock me...."[22] Yet the Beatles were hailed for their "music and influence" and were awarded the Order of the British Empire by Her Majesty the Queen, royal head of the Church of England.

Famed architect Buckminster Fuller, after staying up half the night reading Ferguson's *The Aquarian Conspiracy*, suggested that "the spirits of the dead" had helped her to write it. Laughing, Ferguson replied, "Well, I sometimes thought so, but I wasn't about to tell anybody."[23] Friedrich Nietzsche indicated that the inspiration for *Thus Spake Zarathustra* came as a form of possession. "It invaded me. One can hardly reject the idea that one is the mere incarnation, or mouthpiece, or medium, of some almighty power." It takes little thought to conclude which "power" inspired this great inspirer of Hitler.

Drug use led the Beatles, as it would their fans, into Eastern mysticism and into yoga. They became followers of Maharishi Mahesh Yogi and practiced his Transcendental Meditation (TM) style of yoga. When he first brought it to the West, Maharishi called it the "Spiritual Regeneration Movement." When that didn't take, he changed its name to "The Science of Creative Intelligence," and it exploded, especially among celebrities. Today, however, after the influence of Eastern mysticism over the past forty years, nearly everyone wants to be "spiritual"—but not religious.

1. "Yoga purists bent out of shape over trendy twisted poses," *Mainichi Daily News,* Japan, September 20, 2005.

2. Ibid.

3. Marilyn Ferguson, *The Aquarian Conspiracy:Personal and Social Transformation in the 1980s* (Los Angeles, 1980), 126 (fn).

4. Quoted in Herbert Benson, M.D., with William Proctor, *Your Maximum Mind* (Random House, 1987), 46.

5. "GeoConversation," an interview with Robert Jastrow in *Geo*, February 1982, 14.

6. Dave Hunt, *Occult Invasion* (Eugene, OR: Harvest House Publishers, 1998).

7. Jon Klimo, *Channeling: Investigation on Receiving Information from Paranormal Sources* (Jeremy P. Tarcher, Inc., 1987), 253.

8. William James, "Report on Mrs. Piper's Hodgson control," in *Proceedings of the English Society for Psychical Research*, 23.1-121.

9. Michael J. Harner, *The Way of the Shaman: A Guide to Healing and Power* (Harper & Row, 1980), 20, 42-44, 49.

10. *Magical Blend:A Transformative Journey*, Issue 17, 1987, 13.

11. Copy of confidential report on file.

12. Ferguson, *Aquarian*, 24.

13. For an enlightening discussion not only of Remote Viewing and yoga but of the entire field of psychic/demonic powers, see Dave Hunt, *Occult Invasion*.

14. http://www.militaryremoteviewers.com/cia_remote_viewing_sri.htm; see also Russell Targ & Harold Puthoff, *Mind-Reach* (New York: Dell Publishing Co., Inc., 1977).

15. http://www.biomindsuperpowers.com/pages/SuperpowerSeries4.html.

16. Greg Taylor, "The Mysteries," http://www.grahamhancock.com/forum/taylorGreg_mysteries.php.

17. Criton Zoakos et al., *Stamp Out the Aquarian Conspiracy,* Citizens for LaRouche monograph, New York, 1980, 60-63.

18. Ralph Metzner, *The Ecstatic Adventure* (New York: Macmillan, 1968).

19. http://www.lib.virginia.edu/small/exhibits/dead/western.html.

20. *The Playboy Interviews with John Lennon and Yoko Ono* (Berkeley, 1982), 203.

21. Ibid., 169.

22. *Saturday Evening Post*, August 6, 1964.

23. Klimo, *Channeling*, 313.

~4~

THE CONQUEST OF
THE WEST

Had Western intellectuals and hippies not gotten involved in LSD and other psychedelic drugs, the New Age movement would not have occurred and yoga would not have become so popular. One former follower of Yogi Bhajan became disillusioned at discovering that though highly honored by so many, including the United States Congress, Bhajan was, in fact, a coldly calculating charlatan addicted to money, power, and sex. Looking back on her entrance into the 3HO ("Healthy, Happy, Holy") cult, she writes:

> The very first time as a young teenage hippie I took LSD was the day I learned that there are many, many different states of consciousness and I committed myself to exploring my own mysterious inner capabilities as a human being. Soon after that, I began writing down and studying my dreams, meditating, and I began searching for a teacher. I was attracted to Eastern Mysticism and Yoga because it provided a blueprint for what I was already involved in and it gave me a methodology for inner exploration that was not dependent on drugs....

> It is of course, perfectly natural to turn to people who are more experienced than we are and apprentice ourselves as their students.[1]

Eastern mysticism has now penetrated every area of today's Western society. Children are being schooled in it from their earliest years through comic books, TV cartoons, movies, and videos that feature weird creatures with mind powers that exceed what even science fiction writers imagined a generation ago. Some of the earlier influential cartoons and movies in this category were *Dark Crystal, Thunder Cats, She-Ra, He-man, Karate Kid, Masters of the Universe, Teenage Mutant Ninja Turtles*, and many others. The ongoing success of the *Star Wars* and *Star Trek* series continues to demonstrate the lasting appeal of an impersonal "Force" underlying the universe. Unlike the personal God of the Bible, this "Force," even if it were more than merely a rebellious delusion, would still be incapable of holding man morally accountable. Even worse, it could be tapped into with the mind and used to one's own selfish ends.

Transforming the West through Media

Luke Skywalker's spacecraft in *Star Wars* crashed into a swamp, where it remained because he didn't know how to get it out (an odd fate for a machine capable of zooming through space). That was when Luke met "Yoda," a strange dwarf-like creature of unknown origin, who was able to lift the ship out of the swamp with his mind. How did he develop such power? Change the "d" to "g" in Yoda's name and you discover the secret of his power—yoga, of course, the thinly disguised "meditation" he recommended to Luke.

This belief in an impersonal force that permeates the universe and that mankind can tap into through mystical rites is not new. It has been the underlying belief of primitive religions led by initiates, or masters, variously called shamans, witchdoctors, medicine men, gurus, yogis, etc., for thousands of years. Its utilization by heroes for seemingly supernatural exploits is found in the ancient fairy tales common to all cultures. Nor has our modern world, with its worship of science, been able to escape the myths that seem to be embedded in human consciousness—again, seen planted there by the Serpent's promise of godhood to Eve. The shift in consciousness to which Marilyn Ferguson referred has spawned two major developments, both related to yoga, though the connection may not be apparent to most readers without further explanation:

1. In general, children (and even adults) no longer look upon the fantastic powers exhibited by heroes or their evil enemies in videos and movies as fiction but as something to which they could attain as well if they only knew the secret. No one needs God anymore, because each person has the same God-powers within—it's only a matter of learning how to master them. (Harry Potter has proved that to the new generation.)

2. The Serpent's promise to Eve in the Garden that she could become one of the gods is no longer viewed as a seductive lie that destroyed the human race in separating it from God and bringing His judgment. It has become the new truth, realized by fictional characters who are the new heroes to replace David who defeated Goliath, Daniel who came through the lions' den unscathed—and even God himself.

Harry Potter, an ordinary boy who became a super being/wizard, embodies the belief and ambition of this new generation. It doesn't bother the avid readers of this series that Harry is a self-ish boy, intent upon realizing his every desire at the expense of others. He is their hero, and they cheer his power to control the minds of others. In addition to the *Star Wars* and *Star Trek* series, an entire genre of "fiction as truth" such as *Kung Fu*, *Highway to Heaven*, *Touched by an Angel*, and, more recently, *Ghost Whisperer* and *Medium* (in both of these, spirits from "the other side" communicate information to women who are mediums, who then use the information to assist people in this world), as well as TV cartoons by the dozens, such as *Power Rangers*, *Yu-Gi-Oh*, and Nickelodeon's *Avatar*, have made Eastern mysticism the normal way of thinking. This is a change in consciousness—and its possible consequences for the future are alarming!

Yoga Fits this New "Image of Man" like a Glove

And now we have yoga, brought to the West by yogis who seemingly demonstrate super powers of body and mind, which they offer to others. Hope is held out for health and even long life beyond anything conventional Western medical expertise is able to promise. Even medical science is succumbing to the tantalizing hope:

> Foundations, government agencies, teaching hospitals, and universities are now sponsoring numerous studies testing scientific evidence for the efficacy of prayer.... Perhaps the most comprehensive symposium ever convened on religion and medicine was held in Leesburg, Virginia. Leading researchers...convened to "stimulate an explosion of research in religion in health." The conference was designed to "determine the viability and mechanism of placing 'the faith factor' into mainstream medical care."
>
> A Harvard Medical School study conducted under Dr.

Herbert Benson [author of *Timeless Healing*] found that repetitive prayer and the rejection of intrusive thoughts results in a specific set of physiologic changes that resemble relaxation. This "relaxation response" is beneficial therapy when treating a number of diseases, including hypertension, cardiac rhythm irregularities, chronic pain, insomnia, infertility, the symptoms of cancer and AIDS, premenstrual syndrome, anxiety, and mild-to-moderate depression.

To Benson, any form of prayer is as valid as another— prayers to Jesus, praying the rosary, or using a mantra—as long as the person believes in it. Benson takes this one step further, suggesting that the "relaxation response" and the "faith factor" are "not the exclusive domain of the devout. People don't have to have a professed belief in God to reap the psychological and physical rewards of the faith factor." In other words, you don't even have to be sincere. You just have to pray![2]

Deepak Chopra, himself both a medical doctor and yogi (once a partner with Maharishi Mahesh Yogi and major promoter of TM), writes books that hold out to readers the promise of fantastic powers that Chopra obviously doesn't experience himself. Nevertheless, his books such as *Ageless Body, Timeless Mind* and *The Seven Spiritual Laws of Success*—and even *How to Know God: The Soul's Journey into the Mystery of Mysteries*—have become bestsellers, and his lectures are sold out everywhere.

All across America, Young Men's Christian Associations and Young Women's Christian Associations (which once were truly Christian but are now pagan, yet haven't dropped "Christian" from their names) offer classes in yoga, supposedly purely physical. Churches of all denominations are following the trend, as though yoga were some neutral exercise that could be used to attract and keep new church members. We even have Yahweh Yoga, with "certified Christian yoga teachers."[3] According to Palaniswami, the editor of *Hinduism Today*, yoga and other forms of Eastern meditation "were too sophisticated for public consumption 30 years ago, but today they're the hottest item on the shelf."[4]

Universities have long offered courses in Yoga Psychology, Metaphysics, Hatha Yoga, The Origins of Salem Witchcraft, Eckankar, Tarot Card Workshops, Psychic Development and Techniques, Astrology, Self-Awareness Through Self-Hypnosis, and similar subjects. Sixteen years ago, a *Washington Post* article about a Maryland grammar school was titled "Meditation Comes to the Classroom,"[5] while the *Seattle Times* reported that inmates at Walla Walla State Penitentiary were learning "stress management" through the regular practice of Hatha Yoga.[6] More than twelve years ago, a nationally syndicated columnist wrote:

> Instead of singing hymns, they're sitting in the lotus position chanting "om" at America's oldest school of theology [Harvard Divinity School]. The Nave's [school paper] calendar reminds students that March 20 is…"a special time to listen to the Buddha and meditate on the perfection of enlightenment…." There's no mention of Palm Sunday or Passover, reflecting their insignificance at an institution where all is venerated, save Western religion….
>
> Harvard…is an elite institution, training the next generation of mainline church leadership. Its degrees are passports to power in the Protestant establishment….Will the last graduating Christian please collect the Bibles and turn out the lights?[7]

Life Is an Illusion–So Make Up Your Own!

Much of the blame for bringing Eastern mysticism to the West, especially into Roman Catholicism, goes to Jesuit priest Pierre Teilhard de Chardin. Psychologist Jean Houston (who supposedly led Hillary Clinton into "contact" with the discarnate spirit of former First Lady, Eleanor Roosevelt) was heavily influenced as a young girl by de Chardin.[8] Houston claims that the techniques from transpersonal psychology, which she teaches for activating the imagination, open the person to a new reality. Echoing de Chardin's Eastern mysticism, she claims that this alternate reality is more real than the "cultural trance," known as "normal waking consciousness...in which we all dream the same dream, more or less, and call it: reality."[9] The altered state of consciousness reached under yoga is supposed to provide an escape from this "dream" of normal consciousness.

Carl Jung wrote introductions to some of the first Western editions of books on yoga and Eastern mysticism. Reflecting the Hindu view that life is but a dream, Jung was obsessed with dreams and their interpretation. In one dream, he saw himself in yogic meditation representing his "unconscious prenatal wholeness...." In commenting upon the dream, Jung declared:

> In the opinion of the "other side" [i.e., the communicating spirit guides] our unconscious existence is the real one and our conscious world a kind of illusion...which seems a reality as long as we are in it. It is clear that this state of affairs resembles very closely the Oriental conception of Maya.[10]

Imagine how far one has fallen from the truth and from God to believe the absurdity that dreams are the real life and consciousness is a delusion! Though they were repugnant to common sense, Jung reveled in the multiple communications that he claimed to have received from the "other side." These became the basis for much of the Jungian psychology still practiced in the West, which is especially influential among Christian psychologists! The messages were consistent with the vast majority of such communications—proving again a common source and identifying that source beyond dispute.

Over and over, Eastern mysticism rears its serpentine head, promising the ancient lie: "You are God, and therefore capable of creating any reality you desire, if not now, then in a later incarnation."[11] Again, it is Hinduism's belief that all is *maya*, or illusion. Jean Houston's goal is to deliver us from this common delusion so that

> ...we will one day look back astounded at the impoverished world of consciousness we once shared, and supposed to be the real world—our officially defined and defended "reality."[12]

Can Hatha Yoga Be Dangerous?

Hatha Yoga instructor Charles Muir is a case study of the deceptive persistence in labeling something "healthful" that is really "spiritual"—and without any warnings of the dangers inherent in yoga. He began studying yoga in 1965 at the age of eighteen and, a few years later, became one of only four people in the world approved by TV Yogi Richard Hittleman to teach the latter's "Yoga for Health" method. For ten years, while teaching what was supposedly a purely physical yoga for health, he continued his own studies of yoga under swamis from the East, such as Satchidananda, Premananda, Vishnudevananda, Satyananda, Madhavananda, Ma

Yoga Bhakti, and Yogis Bhajan, Majumdar, Bua, and Mishra.[13] It would be an insult to these swamis and yogis to insist that what they teach is merely physical without any involvement in the spiritual. But how many, if any, would admit to the dangers that lie just beneath the surface?

From 1969 to 1974, Muir was New York City's "Yogi in residence," co-teaching the popular "Yoga on the Green" and "Yoga Day Happenings" in Central Park. Twice he received awards from New York City Mayors (Lindsey and Beame) for "his efforts to advance the spiritual and physical values of Yoga for the benefit of all citizens."

"*Spiritual*" benefits being taught to all New York citizens, most of whom lacked the common sense to inquire as to what religion this eastern spirituality represented? Of course, most of them probably didn't care.

In 1972, Muir was named co-director of the Yoga for Health centers in New York, New Jersey, and Connecticut. From 1974 to 1978, he established and directed the Yoga For Health Schools throughout California and conducted seminars throughout the U.S. and Mexico. In 1978, he founded the Source School of Tantra® in California and Maui, Hawaii, and has functioned as its Director of Studies since then.[14] But where are the warnings about the dangers one finds in the ancient books by the originators of yoga? Why are these dangers not disclosed? Is this false advertising?

Warnings to Heed

In a frank interview in *Yoga Journal*, Ken Wilbur, a yoga expert who is often called the "Einstein of consciousness," warns that Eastern meditation, no matter how carefully practiced, involves "a whole series of deaths and rebirths...some very rough and frightening times."

David Pursglove, therapist and transpersonal counselor for decades, warns that those involved in Eastern meditation can encounter "Frightening ESP and other parapsychological occurrences... out-of-body experiences...[encounters] with death and subsequent rebirth...awakening of the serpent power (Kundalini)...violent shaking and twisting...." The *Brain/Mind Bulletin* warns that "such experiences are common among people involved in Yoga, [Eastern] meditation...." Another expert adds his sober word of warning:

> I advanced in the occult sphere so fast that I soon became the youngest guru in the Western Hemisphere, and one of the most advanced and powerful. Twice a week I taught yoga on television. Hatha-Yoga sounds like a nice simple set of exercises; everyone thinks it is just gymnastics. I want to warn that it is just the beginning of a devilish trap. After I became an instructor in Hatha-Yoga, my guru showed me that the only thing these exercises do is open your appetite for the occult. They are like marijuana; they usually lead you on to a drug that is worse and stronger, binding you so completely that only Christ can deliver you. Many people think that occult power is just the power of the mind. This is not true. There is a point beyond which the power of the mind ends and the demonic power takes over.[15]

Among the few who honestly warn the public is Dr. Walt Larimore. He explains, "Yoga has spiritual roots.... [Therefore] one could argue that promoting it in schools violates the...so-called separation of church and state...." He warns that the "deeply religious practice" of yoga, with its roots in Eastern mysticism, may put kids in a position to be influenced by elements that are not at all healthy.[16]

Consider the following letter, typical of many we have received over the years: "My daughter, age 43, for the past 10 years has been involved with Hatha Yoga and at the present time she is experiencing exactly what you describe in *Occult Invasion*, pg. 225, sentences 9 and 10 ['violent shaking, hallucinations, murderous impulses... uncontrollable rage...trying to commit suicide...']. She says she would like to give up Yoga and be released from the spirit of her last teacher that is currently inflicting excruciating pain upon her. We've taken her to see several doctors, but they have been of no help. Her mother and I are at our wits end.... Please help if you can."

Of course, nothing like this horror was even hinted at by those who taught her yoga as a supposedly healthful daily practice, which was promoted as purely physical. Demonic invasion of her mind and body was the last thing she had in mind when she began to practice Hatha Yoga, but it happened to her—and she is typical of many, many others. It is our hope and prayer that this volume will be the means of delivering many before it is too late.

1. http://www.rickross.com/reference/3ho/3ho19.html.

2. Gary Thomas, "Doctors Who Pray," parts 1 & 2, *Christianity Today*, January 1997.

3. www.yahwehyoga.net.

4. Cited in *Christianity Today*, April 8, 1999, 64.

5. *Washington Post*, May 10, 1990.

6. *Seattle Times*, April 29, 1990.

7. Don Feder, "'Omm' echoes from Harvard," in *Washington Times*, April 19, 1994.

8. Jean Houston, *Life Force:The Psycho-Historical Recovery of the Self* (Quest Books, 1993), 254-56.

9. Ibid., 211-42.

10. C . G. Jung, *Memories, Dreams, Reflections* (Pantheon Books, 1963), 323-24.

11. "The World According to Ram," *The Utne Reader*, July-August 1988, 80, abridged from Martin Gardner, *The New Age Notes of a Fringe Watcher* (Prometheus Books, 1988).

12. Robert Masters and Jean Houston, *Mind Games* (Dell Publishing, 1992), 13, 229-30; see also Houston, *Life Force*.

13. http://www.sourcetantra.com/tantra_credentials.htm.

14. Ibid.

15. Quoted in Colin Weightman and Robert W. McCarthy, *A Mirage from the East* (Adelaide, Australia: Lutheran Publishing House, 1977), 8.

16. http://headlines.agapepress.org/archive/9/62005e.asp.

~5~

BEWARE THE "SCIENCE" OF YOGA

Summarizing briefly what we have seen so far: in a classic flimflam, one of the world's most ancient religious practices is being promoted as "science." For example, Swami Sivananda of Rishikesh, India, one of the most highly regarded yogis to come to the West, declares that Kundalini yoga "is an exact science." Here is part of the description he gives:

> Kundalini Yoga is that Yoga which treats of Kundalini Sakti, the six centres of spiritual energy (Shat Chakras), the arousing of the sleeping Kundalini Sakti and its union with Lord Siva in Sahasrara Chakra, at the crown of the head. This is an exact science. This is also known as Laya Yoga. The six centres are pierced (Chakra Bheda) by the passing of Kundalini Sakti to the top of the head. "Kundala" means "coiled." Her form is like a coiled serpent. Hence the name Kundalini.[1]

One can only wonder which branch of science has verified the nature of this feminine "spiritual energy" that lies coiled like a serpent at the base of the spine and springs up when aroused through the practice of yoga! What science is it that has identified the "chakras" through which the Kundalini force manifests itself? Certainly nothing that would be accepted as "science" in the West. It sounds much like the Westernized Hinduistic cults of Religious Science, Christian Science, Unity, and Science of Mind, which have rejected the personal God who created us and posited instead an impersonal "Universal Mind" that has *no mind* of its own and can be tapped into for personal benefit—a cosmic "energy," pervading the universe, which man can control and use to his own ends.

Look out! Many former yogis, such as Rabi Maharaj, have found this alleged psychic force, which parapsychologists avidly seek, to be very destructive when they refused to submit to it and tried to escape its control. So by claiming that yoga is an "exact science," Sivananda is engaging in gross misrepresentation. What he means is that mysterious alleged psychic powers, indefinable by Western materialistic science, have been found to be available to those who give themselves blindly to the Kundalini serpent and remain in bondage to it until it destroys them. Such destruction has befallen many of the gurus who have gained a large following in the West—such as Rajneesh, Muktananda, and others, as we shall see.

Nevertheless, science is increasingly being drawn by the allure of alleged psychic powers that are promised through Eastern mysticism and are seemingly demonstrated by yogis who have come to the West from India. Under the heading, "DALAI LAMA, TOP SCIENTISTS, TO DISCUSS SCIENCE & CLINICAL APPLICATIONS OF MEDITATION AT MIND & LIFE CONFERENCE AT WASHINGTON, D.C.," the news release declared:

The Mind & Life Institute, in partnership with the Georgetown University Medical Center, and the Johns Hopkins University School of Medicine, will host 'Mind & Life XIII: the Science and Clinical Applications of Meditation,' November 8-10, 2005, at DAR Constitution Hall in Washington, DC. The historic conference on meditation, a convergence of Eastern and Western thinkers, will feature acclaimed speakers from scientific and contemplative communities, among them, His Holiness the Dalai Lama.... The 3-day conference on the cutting-edge of science and meditation, will be only the second public dialogue on this topic with the Dalai Lama, the internationally recognized Nobel laureate and Tibetan spiritual leader.[2]

The "Science of Kundalini Yoga"

Yogi Bhajan's followers claim that it was he who brought Kundalini Yoga "to the West...in 1968." He taught thousands to release this "serpent force coiled at the base of the spine, waiting to spring up through the chakras" by means of yoga. Yet the United States Congress, as noted in the first chapter, feted Yogi Bhajan. In doing so, it honored Kundalini Yoga (in Chapter Seven, we will see how destructive this can be). Known as "The Aquarian [i.e., New Age] Teacher," Yogi Bhajan, too, was anything but bashful in claiming that yoga was a science:

> Men of great knowledge actually found out about the chakras—their workings, their petals, their sounds, their infinity, their co-relationship, their powers. They found that the life of a human is totally based on these chakras. This total science gave birth to Kundalini Yoga.[3]

This faith (yes, it is a very devout *faith*) in the various forms of yoga as supposed science has been successfully passed on to a multitude of devout disciples. Their devotion is demonstrated, as we have seen, in the almost worshipful quotations of their "masters." Consider the following from a popular website:

> Dana is a KRI Certified Kundalini Yoga Teacher and a Professional Member of the International Kundalini Yoga Teacher's Association. She felt an immediate connection to the Science of Kundalini Yoga as taught by Yogi Bhajan. She feels that the divine teachings of the Master, which allow us to tap into a technology of breathing techniques, body postures, hand positions, sound currents and body locks, can manifest into grace and greatness in a person. Dana loves to share the blessing of Yogi Bhajan's teachings in her energetic and soulful classes. She is devoted to Kundalini Yoga taught as the original sacred science.[4]

A *sacred* science based upon *divine* teachings? Did Galileo, Francis Bacon, Robert Boyle, Isaac Newton, Louis Pasteur, or any other great scientist, past or present, ever suggest that they followed a "sacred" science? Were the discoveries of Einstein, Sir James Jeans, Arthur Eddington, or Erwin Schroedinger ever considered by fellow scientists to be "divine teachings"? Were their discoveries ever treated by the academic world as infallible and not to be questioned or even discarded if further discoveries invalidated them? What bogus and dangerous science is this that the yogis are selling? And how is it that well-educated, sophisticated Westerners are buying it in ever-increasing numbers? What could be the reason for this astonishing gullibility?

The "Divine Science of Kriya Yoga"

It would surely create suspicion and be severely denounced by the scientific community if a mathematician or astronomer or chemist or any other scientist or scholar were to slavishly follow the teachings of past scientists and quote them as infallible. But it is normal for those who follow the "science of yoga" to quote the swamis and gurus who initiated them as though they were the gods themselves. One instructor quotes Yogi Bhajan as though quoting the very words of God: "Amid the swirling, confusing, unfocused energies of the modern world, there is a light, a calm and a healing in the center of All things."[5] That "center," of course, according to the yogis, is the Divine Self waiting to be realized within. Parroting the foundational belief behind all yoga, Paramahansa Yogananda, "the first great master of India to live in the West for a long period (over thirty years),"[6] declared:

> We are all part of the One Spirit. When you experience the true meaning of religion, which is to know God, you will realize that He is your Self, and that He exists equally and impartially in all beings.[7]

So God is what I am in my own Self? How many of my friends and acquaintances would imagine that I am God? Why is it that I don't manifest the divine and infinite characteristics and powers of God but rather those of a fallen creature obviously acting in rebellion against the true God? What lie is this—and what incredible delusion blinds those who believe it?

There is no denying the fact that this is the "ancient wisdom" of the Serpent, with which the Bible says he deceived Eve and brought destruction upon the human race. This delusion that men are, or could become, gods permeates the worlds of both science and religion. Paramahansa Yogananda praises what he considers to be the recovery of this "ancient wisdom of the Serpent": "the science of Kriya Yoga...became widely known in modern India through... Lahiri Mahasaya, my guru's guru.... Because of certain ancient yogic injunctions, I may not give a full explanation of Kriya Yoga in a book intended for the general public.... Kriya is an ancient science. Lahiri Mahasaya received it from his great guru, Babaji, who rediscovered and clarified the technique after it had been lost in the Dark Ages."[8] In order to gain wider approval, he goes on to assert, while blaspheming Christ, who neither practiced nor even mentioned any kind of yoga:

> "The Kriya Yoga that I am giving to the world through you in this nineteenth century," Babaji told Lahiri Mahasaya, "is a revival of the same science that Krishna gave millenniums ago to Arjuna; and that was later known to Patanjali and Christ, and to St. John, St. Paul, and other disciples [yet is never mentioned in the entire New Testament]."
>
> Kriya Yoga is twice referred to by Lord Krishna, India's greatest prophet.... Krishna also relates that it was he, in a former incarnation, who communicated the indestructible yoga to an ancient illuminato, Vivasvat, who gave it to Manu [who] instructed Ikshwaku.... Passing thus from one to another, the royal yoga was guarded by the rishis until the coming of the materialistic ages. Then, because of priestly secrecy and man's indifference, the sacred lore gradually became inaccessible.[9]

Hinduism's "Christian Science"

Maha*rishi* Mahesh Yogi, of course, claims to be in that long line of *rishis* passing along the version of yoga he learned from his guru, Dev.

Yogananda brought his style of Kriya Yoga to the West. To propagate it, he established the Self-Realization Fellowship in the United States in 1920, which has spread to over 500 meditation centers in more than 50 countries. The annual conference attracts many thousands of participants from around the world. Today's yoga instructors in the West who franchise their own brands and deny that yoga has any connection to Hinduism are either engaged in a giant cover-up for commercial reasons or are inexcusably ignorant.

It would be a worldwide scandal if even the greatest scientist of all time were spoken of with the reverence we find in the following editorial from a special edition of the *Research Journal of Philosophy* dedicated to "Sri Sri Paramahansa Yogananda":

> We have immense joy in dedicating the present issue of the *Journal* to the prophet, saviour and savant, Sri Sri Paramahansa Yogananda, who sanctified Ranchi [University] by his hallowed presence; and by his educational and spiritual works....
>
> The unique contribution of Paramahansa Yogananda consists in the revelation of *Kriya Yoga* to mankind.... By *Kriya Yoga* the union of the spiritual Self with God can be achieved by an individual.... Elijah, Jesus, Kabir, and other prophets were past masters in the use of Kriya or a similar technique, by which they caused their bodies to materialize and dematerialize at will.[10]

So Christ was just another yogi, a self-realized "Master,"

like the other frauds who claim to be gods but act like selfish, power-mad, sinful men? Christ said, "Which of you convinceth [convicts] me of sin?" (John 8:46). No one could refute His claim to sinless perfection—but the same cannot be said for the yogis, as we shall see.

We have historic eyewitness accounts testifying that Christ raised the dead, healed all the sick, the blind, the lame, etc., who came to Him. We have eyewitness accounts establishing the historicity of Christ's resurrection. He is not just another guru, and He neither practiced nor needed yoga. Christ was and is God, who came to earth as a man through a virgin birth to die for mankind in payment of the penalty for their sins—and that includes the sinful "yogis" who denigrate Him. Tragically, those who claim to be Christians, the followers of Christ, are now denying Him in turning from His life within to seek help from yogis who cannot even help themselves!

A Lucrative Business

Fortunes have been and are still being made by the gurus and by Western proprietors of yoga centers who wouldn't dare to call themselves gurus but pass on the delusion by teaching yoga. The cost of initiation into any form of yoga can often add up to many thousands of dollars. Such is the case, for example, with "Bikram yoga," named after its originator, Bikram Choudhury of Calcutta, now living in the United States. The greatest cost, however, is the loss of one's soul for eternity that often befalls those who become involved in yoga. We urge those who may have—or who are thinking of trying it—to consider this warning very carefully.

Choudhury has become wealthy by patenting and franchising

his brand of yoga, initiation into which generally sells for around $5,000 or more, depending upon the extras. He "argued in federal court that his precise sequence of yoga postures and breathing exercises should be eligible for copyright protection...." That claim "riled the yoga community." Nevertheless, a federal judge agreed that his aggressive stance was "well within Choudhury's rights as the copyright owner."[11]

Choudhury has quite an empire to protect as the source of his wealth and power. There is a "Bikram studio in almost every major city in America." Critics and rivals now know that he will sue anyone who dares to teach yoga without a license. When challenged for living "the life of a star, complete with a whole fleet of classic cars," he replies, "I'm an American yogi!"[12] But what he teaches and has copyrighted, in spite of his own personal touches, is an ancient Hindu ceremony, which, according to the authoritative textbooks, is fraught with spiritual danger.

An Ancient Religious Ritual

Yoga is a *religious* practice, boasting spiritual claims that cannot be verified. For this reason alone, it is dishonest to call it a science. Sivananda declares that "the fire of Yoga burns all Karmas."[13] This is hardly a scientific idea, but it reveals the basic goal of all forms of yoga: to escape the wheel of reincarnation caused by karma. In fact, reaching the state of consciousness that yoga is designed to create is said to be the only way to escape the otherwise endless cycle of death and rebirth through reincarnation back into this life of suffering.

Furthermore, in spite of the minimal variations added by individual franchisers, yoga has remained basically the same for thousands of years. On that count, also, it is a fraud to call any form of yoga a science. The proof of this fact is easily verified. Most books on yoga begin with a list of the succession of gurus from whom the author gained his knowledge. The dedication of Sivananda's book on Kundalini yoga reads:

> OM: **IN MEMORY** OF PATANJALI MAHARSHI, YOGI BHUSUNDA, SADASIVA BRAHMAN, MATSYEN-DRANATH, GORAKHNATH, JESUS CHRIST, LORD KRISHNA AND ALL OTHER YOGINS WHO HAVE EXPOUNDED THE SCIENCE OF YOGA. (Emphasis in original)

Clearly, yoga is still practiced as the ancient rishis and yogis first developed and taught it thousands of years ago. One would certainly not include any of them in a list of the world's great "scientists"! There has been neither scientific verification nor scientific development in yoga over the many centuries since it was first invented. Nor can the fact that yoga is a religious ritual be denied. And to bring Jesus Christ into this long line of "yogins who have expounded the science of yoga" is both blasphemy and fraud of the worst kind! But with the yogis, as with New Agers, it is perfectly legitimate to make up one's own meaning for any word and to fraudulently claim Christ's blessing for the prestige His name brings. This dishonesty then becomes the mind-set of their followers as well.

Choudhury says yoga is "a god" that brings "spiritualism [into] your life."[14] Yet he patented and franchised his particular brand of this "god." Clearly, he has his own invented meaning for the common word "god," and certainly no knowledge of the true God, the

Creator of the universe. Those who involve themselves in yoga, wittingly or unwittingly become followers of a false and destructive "god." Again, this is hardly scientific.

"Gods" with Extremely Bad Memories

The basic belief of Hinduism and of yoga that comes from it is that we are all gods and, at the same time, we are Brahman, the supreme god of Hinduism. Yogic enlightenment is the realization "that thou art," i.e., you are Brahman, the All. Does it not seem odd, however, that we must strive for this realization through the practice of yoga? What odd gods we are, who seem to have forgotten our divinity and certainly have lost our supernatural power. Astonishing though it may be, with thousands of years that have demonstrated man's fallen nature in wars and crimes for which we all ought to hang our heads in shame as members of such a proud and wicked race, the Serpent's lie of the Divine within is still believed!

The "self-realization" to be achieved through yoga will supposedly restore this lost memory so that we "realize" once again our true identity as gods. The grand "awakening" comes through yoga, when at last one realizes that atman (the individual soul) is identical with Brahman (the Universal Soul). If that is indeed man's true identity, how could we have forgotten who we are? The very suggestion is preposterous. And what good would it do for us to "remember" that we are gods—wouldn't we just "forget" it again? Forget it!

Nor do any of the yogis who preach this delusion to their eager followers manifest any evidence that they have "realized" their own godhood, although they promise it to others. Maharishi Mahesh Yogi needs an airplane for flying, in spite of claiming that he teaches his followers how to fly on their own by the power of TM. Swami Sivananda needed an umbrella to keep off the rain; Yogananda traveled slowly by train across the country before commercial air transport was available; and Muktananda lived a secret life of sexual immorality (hardly worthy of an alleged "God-man") and died in 1982.

Nevertheless, all of the ancient texts confirm one another in explaining that yoga was developed as a means of realizing one's own godhood. This is the purpose of all of the physical positions, breathing and stretching exercises, and meditation—no matter what today's advertisements say or what the novice joining his first yoga class is led to believe.

Spreading the Lie

Swami Vivekananda, until then unknown in the West, came to the 1893 First World Parliament of Religions, became its darling, and, as a result, opened the West to yoga. Speaking from that Parliament, here is the message that he brought to the western world. Unmistakably an echo of the Serpent's promise of godhood to Eve, it was so obviously a lie that only blind pride could have accepted it—but millions have, and their number grows:

> Each soul is potentially divine. The goal is to manifest this divine within.... Ye are...holy and perfect beings. Ye divinities on earth—sinners? It is a sin to call a man so...a standing libel on human nature. Come up, O lions, and shake off the delusion that you are sheep.... Ye are not bodies; matter is your servant.... Lay yourselves open to these thoughts, and not to weakening and paralyzing ones.[15]

It is absurd that gods with omnipotent power don't know who

they are or what power they possess! Therefore, "self-realization" and the means by which it is allegedly attained are equally absurd. We are "lions" suffering from the "delusion that we are sheep"? Anyone who buys that fantasy is willingly embracing a lie because they don't want to accept the humble truth. And what a contradiction of Christ's teaching that He is the Good Shepherd and we are His sheep (John 10)!

Vivekananda was a man with a body of flesh that eventually succumbed to death. He died as any man, and his body has turned to dust in the grave. Unable to demonstrate the lie he taught, he nevertheless succeeded in convincing multitudes to embrace that delusion.

It is clear that Hinduism was designed by "the god of this world," the arch enemy of God and man, to undermine the truth of the Bible and to prevent mankind from knowing Christ. Hinduism, however, doesn't usually oppose Christ openly, but subtly. It "embraces" Him as one of the great "Masters" and, in the process, turns our Lord into a Hindu "avatar." Here was the false Christ offered to the world by Paramahansa Yogananda:

> The three Wise Men who came to worship the Christ child hailed from India and named him Isa...a Sanskrit name that became Jesus in the Bible. The star they followed was not a physical celestial body [but] in the spiritual eye located between the eyebrows, which [they] accessed through deep meditation.
>
> Jesus traveled to India, where he practiced yoga meditation with the great sages...during his "lost years" from age 13 to 30....
>
> [Yogananda's book] *The Second Coming of Christ: The Resurrection of Christ Within You*, offers...the deeper meaning of Christ's teachings and their essential unity with yoga,

one of the world's oldest and most systematic religious paths to achieving oneness with God.

The book...the first detailed interpretation of the four Gospels by a Hindu...aims to recover what Yogananda believed were major teachings [of Christ] lost to institutional Christianity...that every seeker can know God...by direct experience through yoga.[16]

Jesus "practiced yoga with the great sages"? Then He must have had a guru, and He would have been under the obligation to pass along the teaching in His guru's name, as do all of the yogis who have come to the West. Instead, far from saying that He had been sent by any guru to teach yoga, Christ declared that His "Father in heaven" had sent Him to die for the sins of the world. That term angered the rabbis, and none of the gurus understood it.

Once again, we have the open admission of yoga's religious nature and its real purpose—in contrast to the false image it has been able to maintain deceitfully in the West. And we have another proof that the claims made for yoga are false. Those who are willing to lie about Christ cannot be trusted in anything else they say.

Ticket to Hindu Heaven

The fact that "self-realization" is the goal of yoga is clearly stated by one of the greatest yogis to come to the West. Nor are these Yogananda's ideas alone but the basic teaching of all yogis, though often unknown to or suppressed by Western yoga teachers. Yoga's popularity continues to grow under the claim that it is simply physical exercises scientifically designed to be beneficial to health.

Many yoga instructors are probably ignorant of the true nature of yoga—but such ignorance would have to be willful. The truth about yoga is readily available on the internet and in numerous books. The motive for denying the truth is not difficult to imagine: it would be very bad for business. Not many Westerners would become involved in yoga if they knew that it lies at the heart of the religion of Hinduism and its goal is simply to "realize" that one is a god, fulfilling the Serpent's lie to Eve.

The average Westerner practicing yoga (and perhaps some of those teaching it) would be surprised to learn that the religious ritual of yoga was introduced by Lord Krishna in the *Bhagavad Gita* as the sure way to Hindu heaven. Nor is it generally understood that Shiva (one of the most feared Hindu deities, known as "the Destroyer") is addressed in ancient Hindu texts as "Yogeshwara," or Lord of Yogis—a title that is also borne by Krishna.

Why are the vast majority of Westerners who are involved in yoga ignorant of such basic facts when they ought to be made aware of them by their yoga instructors? The indisputable Hindu foundation of every style of yoga, no matter how physical or thoroughly Westernized, is carefully avoided. On one hand, to admit its religious nature would drive away most of the customers. And on the other hand, many yoga instructors may be ignorant of the truth, having been deceived themselves. They then pass their own misinformation unwittingly on to their pupils, just as they were deceitfully denied the truth when they first became involved.

Even when its Hindu origin is acknowledged (which is rare), yoga is passed off as having nothing to do with Hinduism as a religion because it can be practiced by those who follow any faith—or none. Hearing occasional references to Patanjali's second-century B.C. *Yoga Sutras*, the Westerner assumes that Patanjali was an early Indian Plato or Einstein. In fact, Hindus regard him as one of their greatest spiritual leaders. Patanjali declared:

> Yoga is the control and cessation of the constant fluctuations and modifications of the mind.... By constant practice and detachment are these activities of the mind-stuff to be brought to stillness—or through deep meditation on the Supreme Spirit.... In the blissful liberation of the soul (the individual self) is the Subject's (the Self's, God's) power established in its own true innate nature.[17]

Thinking they are buying health, millions are unwittingly getting entangled in Hinduism. Believing they are being taught scientific practices, yoga enthusiasts, unaware of the deception, are led into dangerous Eastern religious beliefs and rituals that are designed to introduce them to the occult. Rare indeed is the yoga instructor who mentions, even in passing, the many warnings contained in ancient texts that "Hatha," the so-called "physical yoga," like every other kind, is a "dangerous tool."

"Goddess Power"

Yoga is only one of many forms of Hinduism, a multi-faceted religion with millions of gods. Sivananda's ode to the sexual serpent power of Kundalini, whose awakening is a major goal of yoga, removes all doubt about the ultimate purpose for which yoga was designed:

> During meditation you behold divine visions...smell... taste...touch...sounds...when hairs stand on their roots... know that Kundalini has awakened. When the breath stops without any effort...know that Kundalini Shakti has become active. When you feel currents of Prana rising...when you experience bliss, when you repeat Om automatically, when there are no thoughts of the world in the mind, know that Kundalini Shakti has awakened.

> O Divine Mother Kundalini, the Divine Cosmic Energy that is hidden in men! Thou art Kali, Durga, Adisakti, Rajarajeswari, Tripurasundari, Maha-Lakshmi, Maha-Sarasvati! Thou hast put on all these names and forms. Thou hast manifested as Prana, electricity, force, magnetism, cohesion, gravitation in this universe. This whole universe rests in Thy bosom.
>
> Salutations unto thee, O Mother of this world! Lead me on to open the Sushumna Nadi and take Thee along the Chakras to Sahasrara Chakra and to merge myself in Thee and Thy consort, Lord Siva.[18]

The connection to "Mother Nature" and the goddess worship that is becoming ever more popular in the West is not difficult to see. This is one and the same universal goddess worshiped everywhere, variously known as Isis, Demeter, Arinna, Diana, Ishtar, Astarte, Sophia, Minerva, Aphrodite, Luna, Venus, Iris, the Corn Mother, Gaia, and by dozens of other names. Beginning with the U.N.-sponsored Earth Summit in 1992, Al Gore, Ted Turner, Maurice Strong, the United Nations, and others, have been pushing the concept of Gaia as the foundation for protecting the earth under the heading of "Sustainable Development." Christianity is seen as the enemy because it rejects the goddess who is one with the universe and teaches a transcendent God, who is separate and distinct from the cosmos He created.

When it comes to yoga, the mother goddess is Shakti, the force underlying the universe, the consort of Shiva, the Kundalini serpent power that yoga is designed to awaken for man's salvation.

Not only is yoga clearly *not* a science, but Sivananda's description of Kundalini's awakening betrays it as a doorway into the occult. His words ("divine visions...hairs stand on their roots... you feel currents of prana rising...you repeat Om automatically...")

describe the take-over of the yoga participant by some alien personality. Could it be that the Serpent who tricked Eve is still playing his same mind games with new victims? It is undeniable that the lie remains unchanged. And why not, since it has worked so well in damning so many billions of souls? At least Satan is consistant—he is forced to be by the fact that the truth, which he opposes, never changes.

Westernized Hinduism

New innovations have been dreamed up in the West by would-be gurus born in America who have taken on Hindu names and dress. For example, Jeff Kagel, who was born on Long Island, now calls himself Krishna Das. K.D., as he is popularly known, "is a practitioner of *kirtan*, devotional chanting, which originated as a component of the religious form of yoga known as Bhakti and is conducted by call and response. Chanters repeat short phrases over and over, invoking the names of Hindu gods.... The ancient ritual... as practiced by K.D. and other prominent American performers...has taken on a decidedly Western slant."[19] In addition to the traditional Indian drums, there are electric guitars, violins, and mandolins.

> At a kirtan at the Moksha Yoga Center in Chicago...an altar was set up with candles, fruit, and a picture of Jimi Hendrix.... The chants' Sanskrit lyrics [which not one in 100,000 Westerners would understand] were projected on the wall.... "This is the most happy-producing thing I know right now," says Mark Rubin, a lawyer. "It is a combination of grounding and ecstasy."[20]

"Moksha Yoga Center"? The name is at least honest, but few

students initiated to practice yoga there or elsewhere in the West would have any idea of its significance. *Moksha* is a Sanskrit word that means "liberation" and refers to the escape from the otherwise endless cycle of death and rebirth imposed by karma and reincarnation. It is similar to the Buddhist goal of Nirvana and is indeed the goal of yoga: the final transcendence over the "illusion of dual existence." This is the supposed complete release from any sensation of time, space, and matter that make up the maya (illusion) by which mankind is locked into the imaginary world of physical being separate from Brahman, who is beyond being and non-being. This is the essence of the Hindu religion: the "realization" of the self is actually its dissolution into nothingness, the "higher consciousness" of non-consciousness, the "enlightenment" to be achieved by the "science" of yoga!

True Hindus are not happy with the increasing Westernization that perverts their religion. The founder of the Yoga Research and Education center near Redding, California, complains that the kirtan is supposed to be an "exclusively Hindu practice in which believers praise gods to whom they are devoted." He admits that "non-Hindus or those who do not understand what they are chanting may experience a quasi-religious feeling," but true Hindus "would want to know why divine Hindu names are being used" by non-Hindus.[21] Why, indeed!

How can those who don't even understand the Hindi or Sanskrit they are chanting benefit from it? Yet "Joyce Schmidtbauer, a commercial producer in Los Angeles, says she benefits from not understanding the words." She believes that the sounds themselves "'have power and are prayerful.' K.D. agrees. 'It is the very unfamiliarity of the language that stops the mind.... As my path got deeper, the melodies came out in a more natural way for my incarnation....'"[22]

Obviously, that isn't science based upon facts but unfounded superstition. Who cares? The New Age attitude is, "If it works for you, makes you feel good, or spiritual, or fulfilled, or in charge of your life, do it." Here again, to believe such nonsense, one must make a bargain with death and allow words to lose all meaning. That persuasion rescued President Clinton from moral absolutes, and millions of others imagine they can use the same escape from truth, so why not practice a little yoga to achieve more fully the same end? There are plenty of reasons and our purpose is to explain them.

A Plague of "Spiritual Emergencies"

As we have noted, Hatha Yoga is alleged to be purely for physical fitness and devoid of the mysticism involved in other yogas. Such a claim is clearly false. Yoga is yoga, and all of the positions and breathing exercises are specifically designed for yoking with Brahman, the universal All of Hinduism. If the goal is physical fitness, one should adopt an exercise program developed for that purpose, not one designed for reaching godhood in moksha.

In one of the most authoritative Hatha Yoga texts, the fifteenth-century *Hatha yoga-pradipika* (still available today), its author, Yoga Swami Svatmarama, lists Lord Shiva (one of Hinduism's trimurti, or triad of highest gods, that also includes Brahma and Vishnu) as the first Hatha Yoga teacher. Hindus honor Shiva as "The Destroyer." No wonder yoga can be so destructive!

Terrifying experiences, reported *Brain/Mind Bulletin*, "are common among people involved in yoga, [Eastern] meditation and other [pagan] spiritual disciplines...."[23] Drawing on transpersonal psychology and various "spiritual traditions," the mental health profession in the United States changed its views concerning certain behavior and delusions that it had long considered to be symptoms of mental illness. Instead, in an amazing turn-around of definition, it began to credit these symptoms to "spiritual development."

With increasing numbers of people practicing various types of Eastern meditation and yoga, such crises have reached epidemic proportions. In 1980, attempting to deal with the rampant spiritual destruction, Christina Grof (long-time practitioner of Hatha Yoga) organized the "Spiritual Emergency Network" (SEN) with the support of her husband, Johns Hopkins University School of Medicine professor Stanislav Grof. A leading LSD authority, Grof was co-inventor of "Transpersonal Psychology" with Abrasham Maslow and Anthony Sutich.

SEN coordinates numerous regional centers throughout the world involving more than a thousand professionals who allegedly "understand the nature of 'spiritual awakening....'"[24] They attempt to advise individuals who are experiencing the terrors that almost inevitably (sooner or later) overtake those dabbling in Eastern mysticism.

Promotional material says, "Trained graduate students in the School of Professional Psychology at the California Institute for Integral Studies respond to each caller, providing assistance and educational information regarding spiritual emergence. They can also make referrals to licensed mental health professionals in the caller's area."[25] The advisors are "respectful of spiritual experience, familiar with a number of spiritual traditions, and qualified to work with various areas of difficulty...."

So now (in the enlightenment of this "new understanding") it is considered quite normal that "spiritual emergence" through the "Self-Realization" achieved by yoga should lead to "spiritual emergencies." And what is offered to these tormented souls? Not biblical truth and salvation in Christ, which would bring real deliverance, but the bankrupt theories of psychology that can only deepen their bondage.

1. Sri Swami Sivananda, *Kundalini Yoga* (Uttar Pradesh, India:The Divine Life Society, 1999), Preface.

2. http://www.sliceoflaodicea.com/archives/2005/11/alert_historic.php#. See also: http://www.investigatingthemind.org.

3. http://www.kriteachings.org/k/ky.

4. http://www.pranamandir.com/staff.html.

5. Ibid.

6. Paramahansa Yogananda, *Autobiography of a Yogi* (Los Angeles, California: Self-realization, 1971), inside front jacket.

7. http://www.yogananda-srf.org/aboutsrf/index.html.

8. Yogananda, *Autobiography.*

9. Ibid., 243-44.

10. *Research Journal of Philosophy*, March 1974 (Ranchi University, Ranchi, India), i-ii.

11. Mike Brzezinski, "'Hot' Yoga Burns Bright," CBS News, June 8, 2005.

12. Ibid.

13. Sivananda, *Kundalini.*

14. Brzezinski, "Yoga."

15. Joel D. Beversluis, Ed., *A Source Book for Earth's Community of Religions* (Grand Rapids, MI, New York, NY: CoNexus Press, 1995), 46.

16. *Los Angeles Times*, December 11, 2004, Beliefs Section, special feature on Yogananda's new book.

17. *The Yoga Sutras*, I Pada; IV Pada.

18. Sivananda, *Kundalini.*

19. Michelle Orecklin, "Can You Sing Om?", *Time*, October 6, 2003.

20. Ibid.

21. Ibid.

22. Ibid.

23. *Brain/Mind Bulletin*, July 12, 1982, 3.

24. Stanislav and Christina Grof, "Holotropic Therapy: A Strategy for Achieving Inner Transformation," in *New Realities*, March-April 1987, 11.

25. http://www.realization.org/page/doc0/doc0026.htm.

—6—

"THE GREAT DRAGON...
THAT OLD SERPENT"

The prominence of the worship of the serpent and dragon (a giant serpent with legs) in non-Christian religions is a curious but undeniable fact. In the Bible, the serpent and dragon are both symbolic of Satan.[1] Yet the serpent is the major benevolent figure in mythology and in almost all primitive religions. In Haitian voodoo tradition, for example, the Great Serpent is the fountain of all true wisdom and the creator of the universe, who took the Rainbow as his wife and from that union came blood and all creatures. "And then, as a final gift, they taught the people to partake of the blood as a sacrament, that they might become the spirit and embrace the wisdom of the Serpent."[2]

Voodoo has long been the curse of Haiti and New Orleans, among many other places. Though no match for Islam, it is one of the most frightening and destructive religions in existence. Its ceremonies lead to contact with spirit entities through altered states of consciousness following exhaustive, trance-inducing dancing and/or ingestion of drugs. Yoga was designed to reach the same state of consciousness in a far different way.

The dragon is found on thousands of temples throughout Asia, while the serpent dominates the religion of India. In Hinduism, Shiva the Destroyer, one of the chief gods, the Master of Yoga, has serpents entwined in his hair. In yoga, there is no attempt to hide the vital role of the serpent. One of the well-known positions in yoga is called the cobra. Yoga itself, according to Krishna, one of the earliest yogis (the major figure in the fictitious *Bhagavad Gita*, written about 400 B.C.), is symbolized as a raft made of cobras upon which one crosses waters to enlightenment.

In the temples of ancient Egypt and Rome, the body of the god Serapis was encircled by the coils of a great serpent. Numerous other examples could be given, from the plumed serpent Quetzalcoatl, the Savior-god of the Mayas, to the annual snake dance of the Hopi Indians. Manly P. Hall, one of the foremost authorities on the occult (and himself a practitioner of occultism), has written:

> Serpent worship in some form permeated nearly all parts of the earth. The serpent mounds of the American Indian; the carved stone snakes of Central and South America; the hooded cobras of the Druids; the Midgard snake of Scandinavia; the Nagas of Burma, Siam and Cambodia... the mystic serpent of Orpheus; the snakes at the oracle of Delphi...the sacred serpents preserved in the Egyptian temples; the Uraeus coiled upon the foreheads of the Pharaohs and priests—all bear witness to the universal veneration in which the snake was held....[3]

Honoring the Serpent Today

In Greek mythology, a serpent was wrapped around the Orphic egg, the symbol of the cosmos, showing its dominance over the universe and all in it. Likewise at Delphi, Greece (for centuries the location of the most sought-after and influential oracle of the ancient world, consulted by potentates from as far away as North Africa and Asia Minor), all three legs of the oracular tripod in the inner shrine of the temple were intertwined with serpents. As one further example of the many we could offer, consider the Greek and Roman god of medicine, Aesculapius, whose symbol was a serpent-entwined staff from which came the identifying emblem of modern medicine, the *caduceus*.

In the temples erected in his honor, Aesculapius was worshiped with snakes because of an ancient myth that said he had received a healing herb at the mouth of a serpent. Here, quite clearly, we have the Genesis story turned inside-out: The serpent is not the deceiver and destroyer but the savior of mankind, leaving no place for Jesus Christ—and this savior "saves" with herbs or drugs.

Unquestionably, the major "cure" offered by modern medicine is in the drugs it prescribes. As a result, today's society is becoming more and more dependent upon drugs. Still honored by many in the medical profession and recited when the M.D. is bestowed, the Hippocratic oath begins, "I swear by Apollo Physician, by Aesculapius, by Hygeia and Panacea, and by all the gods and goddesses, making them my witnesses...." It would never be allowed to have a statement honoring the God of the Bible or Jesus Christ repeated at medical schools!

And how is it that yoga, which comes from serpent-worshiping Hinduism, has become so popular with hundreds of thousands who call themselves Christians, as well as in many churches? This is true not only in liberal denominations but also in many churches that claim to adhere to the fundamentals of the Christian faith. Who could deny the contradiction? What is the source of this twisted thinking? Much credit must be given to the yogis. They have managed to sell Hinduism packaged as health, physical fitness, and enlightenment. Posing as favoring Christ while denying Him, the popular gurus from the East somehow manage to conceal their immorality as well.

An Honest Look at the Yoga "Masters"

When we look at the lives of the yogis, swamis, and gurus who have manifested Kundalini serpent power and dispensed it to their followers, it is difficult to escape the conviction that the sordid picture reflects "the great Dragon and that old Serpent." Swami Muktananda, affectionately called "Baba" by his followers, was one of the most powerful of the gurus who came to the West, and was thoroughly evil, according to what many of his former disciples testify with one voice. Muktananda was introduced in the West by Ram Dass (the fired Harvard psychology professor, Richard Alpert, who adopted this Hindu name after his initiation by Guru Maharaji). Muktananda became one of the most popular and influential gurus in America.

Yogi Bhajan, sufficiently masterful at living a double life to be feted by Congress, must have chuckled to himself when he said, with an apparent sincerity that deceived a multitude of followers: "People will see that people who practice yoga are bright and beautiful, calm, quiet, and blissful. They will recognize that the yogic community is sincere, dependable, serving and giving. The future of yoga is bright, beautiful, bountiful, and blissful."[4]

When we look at his secret life, however, we see anything but the "beautiful...sincere, dependable, serving and giving" picture that Yogi Bhajan promised would characterize the lives of his disciples and would thereby draw increasing numbers into Siddha Yoga. And the same is true when we look beneath the surface to uncover the truth about the other yogis, swamis, and gurus—the alleged "Masters" who have manifested the serpent's Kundalini power and dispensed it to their followers. A little investigation reveals that Yogi Bhajan's prophecy is pure propaganda. The disturbing truth brings disillusionment that eventually drives many to leave yoga cults. Sadly, the many shattered lives left in the wake of these gurus reflect Satan and evil rather than God and good.

A Powerful and Deadly Influence

Muktananda was both extremely powerful and incredibly evil. Yet it was he with whom Christina Grof fell in love as her spiritual master and teacher. He apparently deceived her completely. His influence upon her life was enormous. It all sounded so wonderful when Swami Muktananda would say: "*Bhakti* means love, and love is only another name for joy. Joy arises when the restlessness of the mind is stilled. Creating a still mind is called yoga. Through yoga, knowledge arises."[5] But his secret life was the antithesis of what he offered publicly to his followers.

Another key person whom Muktananda deceived was former Harvard professor Richard Alpert, who had teamed with Timothy Leary in promotion of LSD, psilocybin, etc., and, as a result, was dismissed from Harvard in 1963. Unquestionably, his use of psychedelic drugs opened him to the world of Eastern mysticism, as it did for countless thousands of hippies during the sixties and seventies. Alpert studied in India under Maharaji, the thoroughly discredited, self-described Christ-Buddha-Satguru-Avatar-Perfect Master, known worldwide at one time to his devotees as "Lord of the Universe."

The power of occult seduction (and related drugs) is illustrated in the astonishing fact that Alpert, intelligent and highly educated, was thoroughly taken in by this teenage fraud and looked up to Guru Mahara Ji as his spiritual master. Under his tutelage, Alpert became a yogi, promoting various forms of yoga for spirituality and taking the Hindu name, Ram Dass. Maharaji, the pudgy "god," has long since shed his Hindu titles and now prefers to be called "captain" because he pilots his own jet. He lives in seclusion in his Malibu, California, mansion, having retired on the fortune he made as a yogi master and "Divine Light" cult leader.

Nevertheless, it was the newly Maharaji-made "guru," Ram Dass, who then introduced Muktananda to the West. As a result, Baba Muktananda became one of the most popular and influential gurus in America. These gurus are the supposed "holy men" of India; yet they are the very embodiment of thinly disguised evil. Jung wrote: "The carrier of mythological and philosophical wisdom in India has been since time immemorial the 'holy man'...."[6] The lives of most of them, however, have sadly proved to be anything but "holy."

The Deadly Deception Continues

Muktananda died in October 1982. His legacy, which he claimed went all the way back to the feared Hindu god, Shiva, continues through his female successor, Swami Chidvilasananda (Gurumayi), who forced her brother, Nityananda, out of cult leadership. The truth is that Muktananda had picked Nityananda to be his sole successor until his sister's pleadings caused the Swami to make her co-successor. But she was not satisfied to share the throne. An investigator writes:

> In Ganeshpuri at the end of 1985...it was suddenly [and deceitfully] announced that Muktananda had named Nityananda as co-guru for only a three-year period, that the time was up, and that Nityananda was therefore stepping down both as co-successor and as a swami.... Devotees were told to turn in photographs and videos that included Nityananda and to excise all...information about him from their books...that pictures of Nityananda should be burned, because they would bring bad luck.[7]

Having taken over the cult and having forced her brother out, Swami Chidvilasananda now claims to be Muktananda's sole successor. She heads some 550 meditation centers and 10 ashrams scattered around the world involving many thousands of devotees in continuous activities that bring in tens of millions of dollars annually. No one knows how much wealth she commands as the successor of a guru who professed a vow of poverty. An insider who witnessed the transfer of power writes:

> [When] Muktananda died...the worlds of 10,000 Siddha people all over the world were darkened. Just about a year before he died, he named his successor, whom he called "Nityananda." Everyone knew he would be his successor, because Muktananda's teacher, whom he absolutely worshipped, was so named....
>
> Nityananda's sister...cried and moaned until Muktananda also ordained her, giving her the name Chidvilasananda [Gurumayi]. A video was made of the

ceremony...called "The passage of Power." I still have a copy.

After Baba died, the brother/sister team took over.... Two or three times they came as a couple to the Santa Monica ashram. I was made head of security including the bodyguards.... [How odd that a self-realized god should need "bodyguards"!]

Chidvilasananda and Nityananda had a falling-out in 1985. The battle became brutal. She initiated the schism by accusing him of sexual indiscretions. I didn't see why that was a problem, because it was no secret that Muktananda was doing exactly that for years....

Nityananda and my friend, Shankarananda, were "detained..." in the Ganeshpuri ashram in India...until Nityananda surrendered any claim in the SYDA Yoga organization. They both escaped in the middle of the night.... She had gained control of all the administrative and financial assets of Siddha yoga, while he was a refugee with his smaller following.

After she became boss, when she came to the Santa Monica ashram, I was still made head of security....

Sometimes Nityananda would come to Santa Monica for his own satsang, set up in a different location by his own devotees.... Nityananda and one of the swamis were followed by some of her henchmen and threatened. I know; I was with one of the Swamis when it happened. The threats were of physical injury and disrupted satsangs, which happened.[8]

Of course, any fault on her part is denied by Gurumayi, and the movement has prospered under her leadership. Thousands of followers refuse to believe any ill reports, while the words she speaks flow in a river of virtue and inspiration: "The wellspring of enthusiasm is your birthright. It is the whole purpose of your coming into this world. Constantly draw from this wellspring: you will experience your own divinity, your own immense treasure."[9]

The face is one of exceptional beauty, innocence, and overflowing love, but how could the truth beneath the façade be different with Muktananda's successor than it was with him?

Former members who keep up with events declare, "Siddha Yoga creates dependence, not liberation...and requires its members to live in dissociative denial.... Critical thinking and questioning are punished by banishment from the community. Suppression and falsification of truth, submissive dependence [upon] the perfection of the guru, are rewarded."[10] One would never suspect what lies beneath the appealing exterior of serenity, which is all the public sees.

Looking a Bit Deeper

The many Western websites promoting Siddha/Kundalini yoga show beautiful faces of instructors whose words are very enticing. One popular site that offers Muktananda's Siddha Yoga is particularly striking in the smiling faces and loving testimonies it presents. There is much, however, that makes one wonder whether surface appearances are too good to be true. One of the instructors "is unabashedly in love with the pulsating dance of Shakti and Shiva... having explored various aspects of yoga for over 25 years, while academically pursuing studies of oriental philosophy...."[11]

Surely his studies must have taught him that the god Shiva is feared by devout Hindus as "the destroyer," and that Hindus say of his consort, Shakti (also known as Kali, Durga, et al.), "Her beauty is in her terror." And to be "in love with the pulsating dance of Shakti and Shiva..."? That dance ends with Shakti's heel on Shiva's neck!

Sexual abuse, illegal activities, and other forms of harmful exploitation are just some of the concrete manifestations of the submission to the control of Muktananda's successor. Former members refer to "the demand that followers ignore and deny the truth of Siddha Yoga's history...." Some assert: "The dissociative contagion that allows the organization to sweep its history of corruption and abuse under the rug is the means by which evil has always been perpetrated and perpetuated. It is the means by which those who participate in Siddha Yoga become unwitting accomplices to the ongoing deception and exploitation of its members and the public."[12]

The fact that some of the Hindu gurus who have come from India to lead the West into "salvation through yoga" often manifest a remarkable occult power is undeniable. The source of this power is betrayed, however, by the fact that they themselves exemplify the moral vacuum into which their followers often tragically fall. Diagnosing one of the most influential gurus to spend much time in the West, one investigator writes:

> Two apparently contradictory themes thread their way through Muktananda's writings. On the one hand, he urges seekers not to be too credulous.... "To love a Guru does not mean to follow after him saying, 'O Guru, Guru, Guru,'" he writes. On the other hand, he maintains, the only way to escape the bonds of ego is to surrender to a guru...by following his path and teachings.
>
> "The Guru is absolutely necessary for one's life...," he writes. A true guru, he adds, is "not an individual, but the divine power of grace flowing through that individual. That power is the Shakti [Kundalini] that creates and supports the world."
>
> To sustain such awesome powers [says Muktananda], a guru "always practices the teachings he imparts to others. He never breaks his own discipline. He follows strict celibacy." In fact, Muktananda advised his devotees to refrain from sex, too.... "Therefore I insist on total celibacy as long as you are staying in the ashram."[13]

It is now an open secret that Muktananda did not practice what he preached. One former swami under Muktananda (who, to his sorrow, investigated and verified Baba's sexual exploits with many, many young girls) is still unable to come to grips with the truth he desperately wanted to deny. He writes: "...how is it possible for someone to be both a saint and a devil at the same time...? Muktananda remains an enigma to me. He was without doubt an extraordinarily advanced soul, with incredible powers; but he was also a demon in his abuse of that power. How is this possible? I don't know."[14]

Certainly, the horrifying truth about Muktananda and other "holy men" of India can do no less than discredit yoga itself, which they all praise as the source of their lives and power. Lies, hypocrisy, lust, and destructive evil do not originate from anything good. As Jesus said, "A good tree bringeth not forth corrupt fruit; neither doth a corrupt tree bring forth good fruit" (Luke 6:43).

It is not possible to be both a saint and a devil at the same time. That a "devil" might, however, seem at times to be a "saint" is no mystery. The Apostle Paul, who most assuredly did not practice yoga, explained:

> And no marvel; for Satan himself is transformed into an angel of light. Therefore it is no great thing if his ministers also be transformed as the ministers of righteousness; whose end shall be according to their works. (2 Corinthians 11:14-15)

"O Guru, Guru, Guru"

One of the most informative and detailed exposés of Muktananda was written by Lis Harris, an investigative reporter. She documents some of the harassment and threats of violence that Nityananda has suffered. After ousting him, his sister has persisted in the attempt to stop him from carrying on Muktananda's Kundalini awakening through his very small organization. Harris writes:

> The spiritual movement known as SYDA boasts a glittering clientele.... But behind all the serenity lie some uncomfortable, ill-kept secrets—and a less than blissful struggle about succession....
>
> I was firmly turned down each time I tried to find a way past the barriers around [Gurumayi]. Moreover...I could never...even sit in the lobby, without having a smiling man with a walkie-talkie or some soft-spoken facilitator swoop down on me. Many of my inquiries...seemed to be met by an air of secrecy. And after I'd had...a private conversation with a devotee, the contents...were reported to the SYDA staff by someone who had been standing nearby....
>
> Shortly before his death, Swami Muktananda was accused of failing to live up to [his own] principles of celibacy...in a 1983 article by William Rodarmo...based on twenty-five interviews with members and former members of SYDA [that] detailed sexual activities Muktananda was alleged to have engaged in with female devotees, many of them fairly young....
>
> A swami named Stan Trout [also] publicly...accused the...guru of betraying the trust of young ashram women... by extracting sexual favors from them in the name of spiritual enlightenment....
>
> Investigating these claims, I tracked down approximately a hundred ex-devotees, ex-trustees, and ex-swamis, all but a handful of whom...were so anxious not to be entangled with the organization that they would talk to me only if I promised not to use their names.
>
> A few former devotees told me that...those who had long-term relationships with him were known as his

"queens...." Several people pointed out to me that, whatever had happened, it was in a context of reverence so great that devotees used to drink Muktananda's bathwater and worship the trimmings from his haircuts, just as, soon enough, Gurumayi's attendants would vie to sit in her dirty bathwater....

Recently...I spoke with two longtime SYDA meditation teachers with...professional careers as psychotherapists, who...investigated some of the allegations, had sadly concluded that they were true...[and] have now left SYDA....

[There are] disturbing descriptions of strong-arm tactics used to hush up ex-devotees or punish them for disloyalty.... It is this element...that has...continued to shadow the organization, especially in...allegations about the treatment of Gurumayi's brother and co-successor, Nityananda....

In fact, my own experience with SYDA...confirmed some of the things ex-devotees complained about. I have been told repeatedly of the harm I would cause by writing negative things about a "pure path"; quiet efforts were made to discredit me with my editors; a barrage of accusatory letters arrived from a SYDA lawyer questioning...my integrity as a journalist and the motives of this magazine; and...the co-chairman and co-founder of a well-known Madison Avenue advertising agency visited the magazine's offices to...warn that there were "many prominent, many powerful people who are going to be hurt by this piece...."

SYDA insists that Gurumayi is the sole repository of Muktananda's wisdom and power. Nityananda, excommunicated from SYDA guruhood, nonetheless stakes his own, nonexclusive claim to successorship, and believes that... what was given to him cannot be withdrawn or lost.[15]

Contradicting Jesus Christ

Christina Grof quotes highly honored Sri Ramakrishna (1836-1886) who, through yoga meditation, allegedly reached a state of god-consciousness attained by few others and whose "spirituality" remains a powerful influence worldwide. Yet the truth is that Ramakrishna passed along to the world some of the Serpent's major lies: "Sometimes the Spiritual Current moves up like a snake. Going in a zigzag way, at last it reaches the head and I go into Samadhi. A man's spiritual consciousness is not awakened unless his Kundalini is aroused...all religions are the revelation of God in his diverse aspects...different religions give us the pictures of one truth from different standpoints...not contradictory but complementary...all of them lead to the same goal.... 'As many faiths, so many paths.'"[16]

He directly contradicted Christ, who said, "I am the way, the truth, and the life: no man cometh unto the Father, but by me" (John 14:6). It shouldn't be difficult to decide whether to believe Ramakrishna, who agrees with the Serpent in Eden and who had no power over death—or Christ, who fulfilled hundreds of prophecies at His coming and rose triumphant from the grave. We have objective, historical, archaeological, and scientific evidence, along with numerous eyewitnesses, to support the Bible, but nothing of this kind for Ramakrishna or Hinduism.

Furthermore, what Ramakrishna said is clearly irrational. The various religions don't even agree on who God is, on what happens after death, or on the nature of heaven, much less how to get there, so how can all faiths lead to the same place? To say that we are all taking different roads to the same destination may *sound* broadminded, but how can it be broadminded to say that there's only one destination ("the same place") and everyone is going there no matter what path they follow? That idea, in fact, is more narrow-minded and dogmatic than anything Jesus Christ taught. He said there are *two* roads and *two* destinies: heaven and hell. And each person is free to choose to which one he or she will go.

"Unitive consciousness," the sense of being one with the universe, so common in the altered state reached both under drugs and through yoga, is closely related to the pagan belief of pantheism, i.e., that God is everything. By becoming one with everything, one has achieved unity with Brahman, who is the "All beyond being and non-being," i.e., one has achieved "self-realization," or the experience of being god. This ultimate goal of yoga is clearly a delusion when reached. It simply isn't true, for many biblical as well as scientific and philosophical reasons. If "God is all," then *everything* is "God." There is therefore no difference between "God" and a germ or a cat or a rock—so the very concept of "God" has become meaningless.

Transcendental Trickery

Transcendental Meditation (TM), one of the most popular forms of yoga in the West, exemplifies the deliberate misrepresentation that characterizes so much of today's New Age scene, including the promoting, teaching, and practice of all other forms of yoga as well. As already mentioned, Maharishi Mahesh Yogi first introduced TM to the West as a Hindu religious practice. In 1957, he started an organization called Spiritual Regeneration Movement for "religious and educational purposes only." He openly taught (and thousands of Westerners, incredibly, embrace this pagan religion) that TM's purpose was to produce "a legendary substance called *soma* in the meditator's body so the gods of the Hindu pantheon could be fed and awakened."[17] But when the TM form of yoga was excluded from public schools and government funding because it was recognized correctly to be a religious practice, Maharishi quickly deleted all reference to religion and began presenting TM as pure science.

He changed nothing except the labels. Such deliberate deceit shows that Maharishi's morals are on the same level as those of the other Hindu yogis. This deception, as we have seen, like every other form of yoga, echoes the Serpent's seduction of Eve—yet it has been furthered by the many celebrities who have practiced and then enthusiastically promoted Transcendental Meditation. Bob Kropinski, a former TM instructor, explains:

> In 1974 [Maharishi]...completely renamed all the corporations...[under] a new set of Articles of Incorporation, deleting everything that said spiritual" and "religious"...to legitimize the teaching of Hinduism.... Maharishi...began calling God "the vacuum state." He instructed [TMers] in the deception.[18]

Subsequent advertisements dishonestly declared that TM "is not a religion, not a philosophy, not Yoga...involves no change of belief system...." In fact, TM involves all of these, and it is yoga. According to Kropinski, Maharishi told those on the inside:

> It doesn't matter if you lie teaching people...[because] TM is the ultimate, absolute spiritual authority on the face of this Earth.
>
> [TMers] are the only teachers and upholders of genuine spiritual tradition.... They're running the universe. They are controlling the gods through the soma sacrifice.[19]

Deceit and Human Destruction

Former TMers have filed lawsuits asking millions of dollars in damages because of the trauma they suffered through Transcendental Meditation. Kropinski (who won such a lawsuit) relates that people experienced violent shaking, hallucinations, murderous impulses, and suicidal thoughts "as a result of the TM practice." At teacher-training sessions, distraught TMers would complain of flying into uncontrollable rages in the midst of meditation, smashing furniture, assaulting their roommates, and trying to commit suicide. Some have managed to kill themselves, and others have gone insane.

Craig Pruit, an atheist at the time, began to practice the TM style of yoga because he had been promised that it would help him get his life together without having to deal with a personal God. After becoming heavily involved in this branch of yoga, however, he began to have serious concerns. It was a shock to him to learn at last that he was involved in something "spiritual"—the last thing he wanted. As he said in a personal interview:

> Several hundred of us from around the world studied for a month with Maharishi in Europe to become teachers of TM. We meditated eight or ten times a day. It was called "rounding"—and the effect of so much involvement in yoga was at times very frightening.
>
> Some...would see grotesque spirit beings sitting next to them when they meditated. Some were attacked by the spirits. It was all very real, not imaginary in the least. Others would find themselves suddenly overcome with blind rage, even with the urge to murder someone. One girl was locked in a room because her behavior had become uncontrollable. The leaders ignored rather than cared for these people as though the problem would cure itself. Maharishi explained

that bad karma was being worked out from past lives—a necessary part of our journey into "higher consciousness."

I finally achieved Unity Consciousness, which made me the envy of others. However, the initial euphoric feeling that I had "arrived" at one of the ultimate states soon gave way to panic. I had lost the ability to decide what was "real" and what wasn't. I seemed to be the whole universe. There were no categories, no difference between myself and a tree or the sky or another person. I felt that I was losing my mind. Maharishi told me to stop meditating. Gradually I returned to a semblance of normality—but I suffered from frequent lapses into Unity Consciousness, much like a flash-back from LSD.

After coming back to the United States, I worked at Maharishi's International University. My roommate there committed suicide. I was committed to a mental institution.

Another former TM instructor, R. D. Scott, tells of numerous "spirit manifestations" among meditators. These included "visions of floating green eyes...creatures of light floating above the puja table [TM initiation-ceremony altar]." Ghoulish creatures materialized periodically to stare with terrifying expressions at participants.[20]

Refuting the claim that these experiences were merely hallucinations, Scott points out that often more than one person saw "the same procession of spirit creatures simultaneously and without any advance warning...."[21] Such possibilities are not mentioned in the ads and brochures promoting the alleged benefits of TM and other forms of yoga.

Beachheads of Occult Invasion

The rapidly proliferating centers where yoga and other forms of Eastern meditation are taught have become focal points of an occult invasion. Such centers have been described as "the first beachheads secured by the approaching forces...to prepare the human species for its collective awakening."[22] The deliberately orchestrated so-called "changing images of man" through "awakening into higher consciousness" is actually the demonization of mankind in preparation for Antichrist and his world religion. For a fuller documentation of that fact, see *Occult Invasion* by this author.

Consider the case of Maurice B. Cooke. A respected Toronto businessman, Cooke became one of today's most popular channelers of "messages" from discarnate entities. That ability suddenly manifested itself as a result of his dabbling in Raja Yoga. Learning to "still" his conscious mind, he began to receive telepathic messages "dictated from a nonphysical source," which identified itself as Hilarion.[23] Yoga opened Cooke to the spirit realm, exactly as it is designed to do.

The incidence of such "contact" with spirit entities is increasing. Cooke did not seek to become a "channeler." That possibility had never occurred to him. It came on him unexpectedly through practicing yoga. But thousands of others have pursued various forms of Eastern mysticism with the deliberate purpose of entering into what they believe to be a dialogue with the spirit world and with allegedly higher entities. Lyssa Royal relates her story:

> I was trained formally by a highly respected channeler in Los Angeles.... In 1986 I began the deliberate choice of developing my channeling ability in order to access the quality and depth

of information that is presented in our books, *The Prism of Lyra*, *Visitors from Within*, and now *Preparing for Contact*.

The channeling process is simple. I put myself into [an Eastern] meditative state.... Another consciousness (or entity) links...telepathically with my brain and then uses it as a translation device....

While in trance, the entities through me are questioned by author Keith Priest and/or various other individuals attending the private or public gathering.[24]

The communications consistently received in this manner by numerous channelers worldwide have been recorded in thousands of books and videos and are influencing the thinking of an entire generation in the West. The transmissions that Lyssa Royal receives from "several entities who are channeled for our research" fit the usual pattern, which promotes the very same Eastern philosophy taught to Eve by the Serpent. Though uncertain of the true identity of the communicating entities, Lyssa trusts the information they provide. She writes:

In no way is it necessary for the reader to believe the entities are who they say they are.... Use the material presented to stimulate your own search for truth. [This is the way of *truth*? No, it's the path to destructive delusion!]

I have often been asked if I really believe that I channel extraterrestrial entities. I have answered that it is not a matter of belief or disbelief. Instead, the importance lies in where the information and the channeling process takes me in my understanding....

The more I channel her [Sasha, one of several entities], the more real she becomes. If she is simply the product of some undiscovered ability within the human consciousness, then I still consider my relationship with her to be a gift. She has opened doors to the universe for me...![25]

So "Sasha," an entity of unknown identity and motive, promises to open "doors to the universe," and Lyssa, oblivious to the danger, gladly trusts her. In contrast, Jesus Christ said, "I am the door: by me if any man enter in, he shall be saved..." (John 10:9). We know His identity beyond any doubt, because in His birth, life, death, and resurrection, He fulfilled hundreds of prophecies that told of His coming, centuries in advance. We know His motive as well. He proved His pure, selfless love for us by dying for our sins (even for those who mocked, scourged, and crucified Him) and by giving eternal life to all who believe on Him.

Jesus is the door, not to the physical universe that will pass away but to the eternal God who created it and to endless joys in heaven. It is astonishing that millions of otherwise intelligent and well-educated Westerners can be so easily persuaded to reject Christ, who is the truth, and to accept as "truth" information transmitted by mysterious entities whom they are unable to identify. The irrationality of this fact offers further proof of the Genesis account of Satan's seduction of Eve and confirms the universal appeal of his lies. Yoga has been the doorway for many unsuspecting Westerners to make contact with these lying entities—as it was designed to be.

What the Gurus Don't Want Their Followers to Know

There is a consistency in the tragic tales told by former followers of yogis, whether Yogi Bhajan, Maharaji, Baba Muktananda, Swami Satchidananda, or any other. The internet is filled with such reports. The very consistency of these independent testimonies argues powerfully for the truthfulness of the witnesses and points to the fact that yoga itself, of any shade or variety, is the main culprit. It is the cause of the lies, hypocrisy, evil, and cover-ups that characterize at some deeper level all of the gurus who have brought "enlightenment" to the West through yoga. The following account is but an echo of thousands of others:

> I was an eighteen-year-old hippie when I moved into [a Yogi Bhajan] Ashram...looking for a magic that would make my life pure and...heal my damaged spirit.... There are three main tests to a human being's integrity. Will you sell your soul for stuff...for sex or love...for power? Like most humans, Yogi [Bhajan] was way deep into all three. Like most cult leaders, however, power was his favorite high...[and] it was power that really scratched Yogi [Bhajan's] itch. He...never took a student that he didn't feel he could control. Of course, he miscalculated because many of us would eventually prove uncontrollable but for twenty years he manipulated...our psyches quite masterfully...a really awesome con man and magician.... That is what I learned during the 20 years that I lived in a cult (i.e., the "Happy, Holy, Healthy Organization"—3HO)....
>
> Most of us emerged from the sixties' hippie culture [with] the love of the philosophy and mysticism of India running in our veins. We all wanted to learn how to meditate and we wanted to get liberated and we were completely clueless as to how to go about that so we prayed a lot and we relied on Yogi Bhajan to guide us. At times we got very, very high...stoned on yoga, devotion, chanting and vegetarianism.
>
> The most titillating and shocking truths concerning my ex-spiritual teacher [involve] his harem (a harem that most of his students, of course, didn't know he was keeping).... After I left the cult I saw that we had...slavishly commit[ted] to and trust[ed] in a gigolo charlatan and... maintain[ed] an almost unbelievable level of denial....

Yogi [Bhajan] was a master of Tantric [sexual] Yoga.... Within the Tantric tradition of India and Tibet...sexual energy is...spiritual energy.... Yogi [Bhajan's] greatest challenge...was not only to seduce supposedly spiritually committed women into his bed...but to keep them quiet about it for over twenty years.... Two of [his former] secretaries actually slapped him with a sexual misconduct suit after leaving the cult. The case was settled out of court and the women walked away a bit richer. We students still in the cult were told that these women were psychotic and that the case had been thrown out of court by the judge because it was completely ludicrous.

Yogi [Bhajan]...gave us a taste of God in the form of various spiritual peak experiences and made us feel safe, loved and secure. Within the context of the cult any attempt to point out that the emperor was, in fact, doing a nude floor show behind our backs, simply would not have been and was not believed. To risk even considering such a possibility was to invite shame and cynicism to come crashing into our lives negating all the magic and hope that we had.... [26]

A "taste of God" and "spiritual peak experiences" through a "really awesome con man and magician"? In spite of the raw evil that this former disciple discovered was emanating from Yogi Bhajan, she still remains under the power of the Serpent. What "God" or "spirituality" could a "con man" offer except the deadly delusion of a satanic lie?

A Consistent Pattern of Evil

There is no denying the shattering truth that many if not most gurus who came to the West promoting enlightenment through yoga, and publicly claiming to be celibates, have carried on secret sex lives that could only be described as a manifestation of powerful and seemingly irresistible evil. Behind the façade and hidden from the public, Muktananda, like Yogi Bhajan and so many others, was a sexual predator who satisfied his lust on young girls and others who came to his ashrams and trusted him as a god. This was often done under the guise of initiating his victims into tantric (sexual) yoga. Highly revered Mahatma Gandhi satisfied his sexual perversion by giving enemas every morning to the young women in his ashram. Although claiming to deny any desire for material things, the wealth various gurus have amassed in the West is enormous.[27]

Underneath it all, what could be the source of this consistent pattern of wickedness except the serpentine Kundalini power, which is the treasured prize the yogis seek? Baba called his method for awakening the Kundalini, "Siddha Yoga," the name of the yoga organization he started in 1961. "The aim of Siddha Yoga is to help every human being realize and experience that they and all other humans have an inner Self which is perfect and divine [i.e., to realize that one is God], and that a reachable goal is the end of human suffering and the attainment of supreme bliss [through yoga, of course]."[28] Here we have another echo from the mouth of the Serpent himself.

If one puts "leaving Siddha Yoga" into Google, nearly 36,000 responses appear. These are mostly the scandalous and tragic stories of former disciples of Muktananda, who report "sexual abuse by [him] and other Siddha Yoga leaders...[such as Yogi Bhajan]." Those posting the stories have done so in order to show beyond dispute that Siddha Yoga ultimately wields an evil influence in the lives of all who practice it.

And yet the seduction continues unabated. In fact, it grows

worldwide. In spite of the testimonies of so many former devotees of various gurus about the evil behind the popular yogis and their organizations, almost all of today's Johnny-come-lately yoga enthusiasts refuse to believe the truth or simply don't care, because they are so sure that they are being helped emotionally, physically, or spiritually by the yoga they practice. Ah, but that was also true at one time (for some of them for many years) of those who have had their eyes opened and now testify of the evil in yoga as they attempt to rescue others.

Yoga opens the door not to true enlightenment but to demonic seduction of mankind. And in spite of the literally hundreds of exposés by those who have experienced the evil firsthand and barely escaped, yoga is gaining adherents among Christians and is being practiced in a growing number of churches, including those that claim to be evangelical. Christian leaders have naïvely encouraged this deadly practice. Robert Schuller was one of the first to give it his endorsement:

> A variety of approaches to meditation...is employed by many different religions as well as by various nonreligious mind-control systems. In all forms...TM, Zen Buddhism, or Yoga...the meditator endeavors to overcome the conscious mind.... It is important to remember that meditation in any form is the harnessing, by human means, of God's divine laws....
>
> Transcendental Meditation or TM...is not a religion nor is it necessarily anti-Christian.[29]

Like so many other church leaders today, Schuller has abandoned the clear teaching of Christ in His Word and advocates any religion that pretends to be "positive"—an idea that has drawn multitudes of Christians into yoga.

No matter what the various schools and forms of yoga being practiced in the West, however, there is no mistaking that if one is interested in true yoga, one must be willing to have that terrifying Kundalini aroused. What is this serpentine power that allegedly lies coiled at the base of the spine? We turn to that next.

---

1. Revelation 12:9.

2. Wade Davis, *The Serpent and the Rainbow* (Warner Books, 1985), 213-14.

3. Manly P. Hall, *The Secret Teachings of all the Ages: An Encyclopedic Outline of Masonic, Hermetic, Qabbalistic and Rosicrucian Symbolical Philosophy* (Los Angeles: The Philosophical Research Society, Inc., 1969), sixteenth ed., LXXXVII-LXXXVIII.

4. http://www.kundaliniyoga.com/clients/ikyta/webshell.nsf/ WebParentNavLookup//2DB48EF3856D82287256SA090079DC7A ?OpenDocument.

5. http://www.pranamandir.com/staff.html.

6. C. G. Jung, trans. R.F.C. Hull, *Psychology and the East* (Princeton, NJ: Princeton University Press, 1978), 177.

7. http://www.ex-cult.org/Groups/SYDA-Yoga/leave.txt.

8. http://www.itisnotreal.com/practices.html.

9. http://www.pranamandir.com/staff.html.

10. http://leavingsiddhayoga.net.

11. http://www.pranamandir.com/staff.html.

12. http://leavingsiddhayoga.net.

13. Lis Harris, "O Guru, Guru, Guru," *The New Yorker*, November 14, 1994.

14. http://www.leavingsiddhayoga.net/abhayananda_st.htm.

15. Harris, "O Guru."

16. www.ramakrishna.org/rmk.htm.

17. Art Kunkin, "Transcendental Meditation on Trial, Part Two," in *Whole Life Monthly*, September 1987, 14-15.

18. Ibid., 17.

19. Ibid., 15-17.

20. R. D. Scott, *Transcendental Misconceptions* (San Diego, 1978), 37-38, 115-29.

21. Ibid., 119.

22. Ken Carey, *The Starseed Transmissions: Living in the Post-Historic World* (Harper Collins, 1991), 54-55.

23. Maurice Cooke, *The Nature of Reality: A Book of Explanations* (Marcus Books, 1979), ix.

24. Lyssa Royal and Keith Priest, *Preparing for Contact: Metamorphosis of Consciousness* (Royal Priest Research Press, 1994), vii-viii.

25. Ibid., vii-ix.

26. http://www.rickross.com/reference/3ho/3ho19.html.

27. www.leavingsiddhayoga.net.

28. http://en.wikipedia.org/wiki/Siddha_Yoga.

29. Robert Schuller, *Peace of Mind through Possibility Thinking* (Fleming H. Revell, 1977), 131-32.

–7–

YOGA'S KUNDALINI "SERPENT POWER"

We have seen more fully in the last chapter the amazing fact that the dragon and the serpent have been worshiped and honored all over the world for thousands of years and are still honored today. The source of the power of the incredible deception behind this strange affection is declared in the Bible in a passage that could be referring to the past when Satan came to the Garden of Eden—and certainly refers to a final event yet future:

> And there was war in heaven: Michael [the archangel] and his angels fought against the dragon...and his angels.... And the great dragon was cast out, that old serpent, called the Devil, and Satan, which deceiveth the whole world...was cast out into the earth, and his angels were cast out with him. (Revelation 12:7, 9)

To summarize what we have documented thus far, in spite of the advertisements and talk about health and fitness, yoga's real goal is to awaken the Kundalini power, coiled like a serpent at the base of the spine, ready to spring up to manifest itself through the alleged "chakras" (centers of the universal force) of the body. The texts by ancient yogis warn that the "Kundalini serpent force" often manifests itself in frightening and destructive ways. Unfortunately, those texts are scarcely known to yoga enthusiasts today and are certainly not heeded by their instructors.

The Serpent's Promise

Kundalini is the "enlightenment" that the practice of yoga is designed to "awaken." One yoga enthusiast writes, "The cobra that opened its fan over Buddha's head is the metaphor for the field of energy, which, other mystics report, emits out from the head during and after sustaining the Kundalini. There are hundreds of religious metaphors for the process when the serpent (sexual) energy is raised to the head."[1]

Might the promise of this godlike "serpent power" be the same promise with which the Serpent deceived Eve by offering her godhood? Certainly, the "self-realization" of "oneness with the universe" and with Brahman, which is the promise of yoga, is at least an unmistakable echo of the Serpent's lies in the Garden. Another enthusiast links Kundalini to "spiritual disciplines":

> *Kundalini yoga* concentrates on psychic centers or *chakras* in the body in order to generate a spiritual power, which is known as *kundalini* energy.
>
> *Kundalini* is the potential form of *prana* or life force, lying dormant in our bodies. It is conceptualized as a coiled up serpent (literally, "*kundalini*'" in Sanskrit is "coiled up") lying at the base of our spines, which can spring awake when activated by spiritual disciplines."[2]

Typical of hundreds of others, another popular website declares: "Kundalini Yoga is the most powerful Yoga ever known and is considered as the mother of all the styles of Yoga. It centers on awakening the Kundalini...serpent power.... Kundalini Yoga was brought to the West by Yogi Bhajan in 1969.... Kundalini Yoga rewards Yogis with spiritual transformation and unity consciousness."[3] Again, we have the open admission of the "spiritual" nature and goal of yoga and its relationship to the Serpent. What could have influenced Congress to commend this to the world?

"Spiritual awakening" through arousal of Kundalini force coiled at the base of the spine is the promise of yoga. But the awakening in the Bible is to truth, wisdom, understanding, and eternal salvation—something that "energy," whether of Kundalini or any other kind, can no more give than can a bolt of lightning. The emphasis in Scripture is upon *knowing truth*, not *feeling ecstasy*. God declares, "Let him that glorieth glory in this, that he understandeth and knoweth me..." (Jeremiah 9:24). Likewise, Jesus said, "If ye continue in my word, then are ye my disciples indeed; and ye shall know the truth, and the truth shall make you free" (John 8:31-32). Of course, there should be feelings, but only based upon the truth. Love is not a feeling that comes from a magic touch. Love is directed to God and others as a result of knowing Him and His love for us.

The "Serpent" and Yoga

In *Up With Eden*, Ken Wilbur points out that in religions around the world, the serpent has consistently been portrayed as the symbol of perennial wisdom and eternal life. There can be no doubt that the Serpent who came to Eve is identified everywhere (except in the Bible) with the occult and is honored as embodying that mysterious force that occultists of all kinds seek to enlist in the accomplishment of their selfish desires. The Bible alone identifies the serpent with Satan and declares that those who seek his occult powers will eventually find themselves entrapped as his slaves and lose their souls. Both the Bible and the occult world of Eastern mysticism (of which yoga is a major part) agree that the serpent represents a very real and powerful spirit being—they only disagree on whether that being is man's friend or foe.

It seems incredible that in spite of the almost universal revulsion with which serpents are held—and in spite of the biblical identification of Satan as "that old serpent, called the Devil, and Satan, which deceiveth the whole world" (Revelation 12:9)—this slippery, repulsive, deadly enemy of mankind is highly honored in nearly all religions. Yoga, as we have seen, is no exception. Nor does Satan shrink from being identified as a snake, in spite of the fact that to call someone a "snake" is to deliver the ultimate insult.

The deception is obviously very powerful. Either the Bible is false in all it says, or what these intelligent and highly educated people are experiencing is the very power of Satan, which Scripture says will be turned loose in the Last Days because of the hardness of men's hearts against the true God. As Paul declared, "Now the Spirit speaketh expressly, that in the latter times some shall depart from the faith, giving heed to seducing spirits, and doctrines of devils..."(1 Timothy 4:1). Could the Apostle Paul, in this prophecy of the Last Days, have been referring to the very delusion with which many gurus have led astray otherwise intelligent and educated Westerners, some of whom grew up in Sunday schools and had some knowledge of the Bible but have turned from that faith to follow doctrines of demons?

Awakening Kundalini

Christina and Stanislav Grof (to whom we referred in Chapter Four as the founders of The Spiritual Emergency Network—SEN) co-edited a book titled *Spiritual Emergency: When Personal Transformation Becomes a Crisis.* Instead of suggesting that there must be something greatly amiss with any transformation that causes a "crisis," the book contains fourteen papers by doctors and other experts on the following types of spiritual crises:

> 1. The shamanic crisis; 2. Awakening of kundalini; 3. Episodes of unitive consciousness ("peak experiences"); 4. Psychological renewal through return to the center; 5. The crisis of psychic opening; 6. Past-life experiences; 7. Communications with spirit guides and "channeling"; 8. Near-death experiences; 9. Experiences of close encounters with UFOs; 10. Possession states.[4]

Surely, any practice that leads to "possession states" ought to be avoided! But transpersonal psychologists today treat all these and other "crises" as normal occurrences along the journey to "psychic opening and personal spiritual growth." Yoga is supposedly a shortcut to this goal. Clearly, something is radically wrong!

Promoting their book, the Grofs' website declares: "Spiritual experience can feel like bliss, but it can also feel like hell. It can cause hallucinations, seizures, pain, panic attacks, mania, severe depression—all the symptoms of physical and mental illness. When people suffer this way, they may feel like they're going crazy, and their doctors may agree. But the authors of this book think that in many cases, such a diagnosis is mistaken. They urge the adoption of a new category of clinical diagnosis, 'spiritual emergency.'"

Incredibly, it doesn't seem to occur to these people that yoga itself and related Eastern mystical practices are the *cause* of these horrifying "spiritual emergencies." Christina Grof has apparently found nothing wrong with the Siddha Yoga of her now deceased idol, Baba Muktananda, being apparently blind both to the personal evil of this man and to the destruction about which the yogis in the East have warned from the practice of yoga for thousands of years. Those ancient Hindus knew nothing of Christianity and the deliverance it brings from sin and Satan, but today's psychologists, raised in the West where the gospel of Jesus Christ is openly proclaimed, have no excuse.

Why the Trauma?

Why should "personal spiritual transformation" create a crisis that could even drive one mad? Obviously, there must be something fundamentally wrong with any method of "spiritual transformation" that leads to crises of such proportions. Westerners accept as desirable and "non-religious," or at least "religiously neutral," the mystical sense of "oneness with the universe" that the breathing and physical positions in yoga are designed to induce. A little honest reflection, however, would tell anyone that there are distinct categories of existence, and that it would be a huge step downward for an intelligent human to unite with earth, sun, and stars, or even with some alleged impersonal universal power. The delusion is akin to Eve's acceptance of the Serpent's lie that she could become a god by eating some fruit.

Those who seek self-realization in the form of unity consciousness end up hugging trees in their attempt to be "one with nature." They would be quickly enlightened (but unfortunately too late) if they tried to pray to a hurricane or "unite" with a river of flowing lava! The professional psychologists involved in SEN as "crisis counselors," who boast that they have "investigated the stages and characteristics of spiritual growth," are blinded to the obvious truth by their prejudice against Jesus Christ and the Bible. Clearly, the problem is a willful rejection of the "Spirit of truth" (John 16:13) in order to follow Satan, the father of lies (John 8:44), whom the Bible describes as "the spirit that now worketh in the children of disobedience" (Ephesians 2:2).

What a contrast these "spiritual emergencies" present to the experiences of the men and women of God whose lives are recorded in the Bible! Christ gives peace and rest, not inner turmoil and terror. For his loyalty to Christ, Paul suffered beatings with thick rods, scourgings with the cat-of-nine-tails, shipwrecks (a full day and night he spent swimming for his life with nothing to hold onto), imprisonments, being stoned and left for dead, etc. Yet he never had a "spiritual crisis" like those commonly experienced by practitioners of yoga and other forms of Eastern mysticism. Instead, in all his trials he remained joyful and triumphant. Paul declared, "Rejoice evermore. Pray without ceasing. In every thing give thanks..." (1 Thessalonians 5:16-18).

From prison, under false accusation and facing death, Paul wrote, "Rejoice in the Lord always.... Be [anxious] for nothing; but in everything by prayer...with thanksgiving let your requests be made known unto God. And the peace of God, which passeth all understanding, shall keep your hearts and minds through Christ Jesus" (Philippians 4:4-7). The Holy Spirit fills the Christian with "love, joy, peace, longsuffering, gentleness, goodness, faith, meekness, temperance..." (Galatians 5:22-23).

It would put the SEN psychologists (and all other psychologists as well) out of business if their clients met Jesus, so they must oppose the truth of God in order to justify their profession. Jesus Christ offers not only to forgive our sins by having paid the penalty that Infinite Justice demanded but to live in our hearts. Nor does Christ, who indwells those who believe in Him, allow any "spiritual crisis" in those whose life He has become—and Christ certainly needs no psychological counseling! The Christian only needs to allow Christ to live His life in him or her.

A Common Source of Delusion

It is no coincidence that the same experiences that assault the consciousness in yogic trance are quite common among users of psychedelic drugs such as LSD. Both create altered states of consciousness, which, as we have already explained (according to neuroscientists), loosen the normal connection between the human spirit occupying that body and the brain. With the normal connection loosened, another "spirit" can interpose itself and tick off the neurons in the brain, thereby creating a universe of delusion that is indistinguishable from real life to the subject experiencing it. Thus, several LSD users who have all "dropped acid" together may at times all experience the same mind adventures simultaneously. Here is proof that the delusion they are experiencing independently of each other, and yet together, has a common source outside of the brain—obviously an intelligent source that can create in the minds of those open to it what seem to be out-of-body experiences, UFO encounters, dying and rebirth episodes, and other mystical events.

Muktananda was the master of Kundalini, who "awakened" it for multitudes, or so they thought. As we have seen, he franchised it as Siddha Yoga. A former bodyguard for Baba, and one-time head of security for his successor, testified:

The purported purpose of Siddha Yoga was to awaken the Kundalini energy, which, through its subtle upliftment, caused the sweetness and bliss I felt and a gradual purification and eventual recognition that the self was everything, bliss and love. I never heard anyone talk about the disappearance of self, only about filling the self with love.

People were always talking instead about their experiences, such as seeing lights, feeling ecstatic bliss during meditation, or seeing Baba coming as a vision in a dream and imparting some special something.[5]

The purpose of the mystical and ecstatic experiences is to draw the seeker further into the morass of evil that eventually claims the soul for eternity. Some escape, but not many. The influence is powerful, like being drugged, and there seems to be a point of no return beyond which only those who truly cry out to the God of the Bible ever recover.

LSD, Mysticism, and Yoga

In 1956, while still in Prague, Stanislav Grof became a voluntary subject in a psychiatric study that required him to ingest LSD. He writes:

My first LSD session was an event that...profoundly changed my professional and personal life. I experienced an extraordinary encounter and confrontation with my unconscious psyche.... This day marked the beginning of my radical departure from traditional thinking in psychiatry.... I could not believe how much I learned about my psyche in those few hours.... I was hit by a radiance that seemed comparable to the...supernatural brilliance that according to Oriental scriptures appears to us at the moment of death [which] catapulted me out of my body. I lost first my awareness of the research assistant and the laboratory, then the psychiatric clinic, then Prague, and finally the planet. My consciousness expanded at an inconceivable speed and reached cosmic dimensions.... The Divine took me over in a modern laboratory in the middle of a serious scientific experiment conducted in a Communist country with a substance produced in the test tube of a twentieth-century chemist.[6]

Clearly, the delusion must be very powerful for an intelligent man involved in "scientific experiments" to believe that the delusive state induced by drugs could ever be the source of truth about *anything*, yet this was what Carl Jung came to accept, as did Freud (a cocaine user) and many others. The ultimate end for all of them has been destructive, as history records.

He seems to imagine "the Divine" as some force underlying the universe. Grof's "encounter with his psyche" under the influence of LSD presents quite a contrast to the sans-drugs sober revelations received by the forty proven prophets who were inspired to write the Bible over a period of some 1,600 years.

Although most of the biblical prophets never knew one another and lived in different cultures and times in history, the Bible is a single book, with each part in perfect agreement with all of the rest. Instead of being influenced by a "Divine Force" and learning about their own psyches in an altered state, the writers of the Bible all claimed conscious revelation from the One True God, Creator of the universe. In fact, the personal, loving God who inspired the Bible condemns the use of drugs, which He calls "sorcery."[7]

For Grof, this LSD trip was the beginning of what he calls "a fantastic intellectual, philosophical, and spiritual adventure that has lasted" more than forty years to the present time. He goes on to explain that under subsequently higher doses of LSD, he had mental "experiences that were indistinguishable from those described in the ancient mystical traditions and spiritual philosophies of the East. Some of them were powerful sequences of psychological death and rebirth. Many clients also reported visions of deities and demons from different cultures and visits to various mythological realms. Among the most astonishing occurrences were dramatic and vivid sequences that were subjectively experienced as past-incarnation memories."[8]

"Past-incarnation memories"? Yoga is inseparable from the theory of reincarnation. This is one of the most obvious lies that the demonic world has produced, as we will see. The theory of reincarnation will be dealt with in the final chapter.

The Psychedelic Connection

For a number of years, Grof, sinking ever deeper into occult delusion, devoted his life to "psychedelic work with patients of various clinical diagnoses." He believed that the records he kept mapped out new territory for Western psychiatry. Then he realized that he had merely "rediscovered what Aldous Huxley experienced [under the influence of mescaline, as we've already mentioned] and called 'perennial philosophy,' an understanding of the universe and of existence that has emerged with some minor variations again and again in different countries and historical periods." This is the "understanding" that multitudes have come to through the practice of yoga—and it agrees with the psychedelic experience. Moreover, as we have seen, it coincides precisely with the occult philosophy with which the Serpent seduced Eve.

Why should Huxley, Grof, or anyone else believe that drugs open the door to a "higher reality" when experts in that field say that drugs destroy normal brain function? In fact, such thinking is a dangerous delusion. Psychiatrist Peter R. Breggin, one of the world's foremost authorities on psychedelic drugs, declares:

> Psychiatric drugs do not work by correcting anything wrong in the brain.... There are no known biochemical imbalances and no tests for them. That's why psychiatrists do not draw blood or perform spinal taps to determine the presence of a biochemical imbalance in the patients. They merely observe the patients and announce the existence of the imbalances... to encourage patients to take drugs.
>
> Ironically, psychiatric drugs cause rather than cure biochemical imbalances in the brain. In fact, the only known biochemical imbalances in the brains of patients...are brought about by the psychiatrists themselves through the prescription of mind-altering drugs.
>
> Psychiatric drugs "work" precisely by causing imbalances in the brain—by producing enough brain malfunction to dull the emotions and judgment or to produce an artificial high....
>
> ...nearly all psychiatric symptoms, including...hallucinations and delusions, can be produced by these drugs.... Unfortunately, drugs that affect the brain and mind can seriously impair your mental function before you recognize that anything is the matter.... If you feel euphoric or "high" from taking the drugs, you may think that you are doing "better than ever" when, in fact, your judgment has been impaired.... [Eventually] the brain places itself in a state of imbalance in an attempt to prevent or overcome overstimulation by the drugs....
>
> In its attempts to overcome the effects of psychiatric drugs, the brain becomes distorted in its functioning. And as already emphasized, the brain cannot immediately

recover its original functions once the drugs are stopped. In some cases, the brain may never recover.[9]

Unaware of the deception he had succumbed to, and of which he had become a major promoter, Grof declared that the "different systems of yoga, Buddhist teachings, the Tibetan Vajrayana, Kashmir Shaivism, Taoism, Sufism, Kabbalah, and Christian mysticism are just a few examples" of this so-called "perennial wisdom."

Once again, we have yoga explained as a religious/mystical practice with roots sunk deep into religious occultism worldwide. This is exactly what one would expect if the Genesis account of Satan's seduction of Eve through the promise of godhood were true. Indeed, the primary lies the Serpent told Eve are commonly experienced by practitioners of all mystical experiences in every culture and time in history worldwide: (1) God is an impersonal force rather than personal; (2) death is unreal; (3) mankind possesses an innate ability to achieve godhood; and (4) "enlightenment" is the doorway thereto.

Yoga, Psychology, and the "New Age"

In the early days of his experimentation, Grof found little sympathy among his colleagues in Czechoslovakia for his new passion to explore and learn from altered states of consciousness. The academic side of the psychiatric world was not yet ready to face the unsettling truth of entering, through drugs, a nonphysical realm that was apparently as real as the material universe. But in 1967 he received a scholarship that allowed him to move to the United States to carry on his "psychedelic research at the Maryland Psychiatric Research Center in Baltimore." On his subsequent lecture tours in America he "connected with many colleagues—consciousness researchers, anthropologists, parapsychologists, thanatologists, and others—whose work resulted in a scientific perspective that resembled or complemented [his] own."[10]

It was at New Age mecca, Esalen, in the Big Sur south of San Francisco, that Grof met Abraham Maslow and Anthony Sutich, with whom he founded the new field of Transpersonal Psychology. It was there also that he met his wife-to-be, Christina. She had experienced—twice in childbirth and once in an auto accident—some of the very states of consciousness that were Stanislav's passion to explore. Her experiences included (without the use of drugs) uncontrollable shaking, visions of white light, feelings of union with the universe, and of dying and rebirth, just as Stanislav and his early patients had encountered under the influence of LSD.

These experiences continued to become more intense through the spiritual exercises she engaged in under the direction of Hindu guru, Baba Muktananda. In his many trips from India to the West, Muktananda initiated many thousands into the practice of Siddha Yoga, just as Yogi Bhajan was doing. Apparently manifesting an even greater spiritual power, however, "Baba" could send a person off into an altered state of consciousness through "Shaktipat," a mere touch with his hand or feather.

As we have already seen, Shakti (after whom this mysterious power is called) is one of the names of the terrifying female Hindu goddess also known as Kali and Durga, who has garlands of freshly-severed hands around her body and drinks human blood from a fresh skull. Her world-famous temple in Calcutta reportedly has the bodies of sacrificed virgins, as required, entombed in its foundation. Christina describes her meeting with Muktananda, the dispenser of Shakti's power, as "like falling in love or meeting a soul mate."

She describes her first experience of *Shaktipat*: "Suddenly I felt as though I had been plugged into a high-voltage socket as I started to shake uncontrollably...a multitude of visions flooded my consciousness...I experienced...being born...death...pain and ecstasy... love and fear.... The genie was out of the bottle...my whole life changed.... I was increasingly impelled by some unknown inner force to meditate and practice yoga, and I recognized Muktananda as my spiritual teacher."[11]

After reading about Stanislav's thousands of experiments with LSD, Christina (who had not used LSD) commented, "...the descriptions I was reading [of LSD "trips"] exactly matched many of my spontaneous experiences of birth, death, rebirth, and spirituality as well as the wide range of emotions and physical sensations."[12] The means of achieving the altered state (crisis, terror, drugs, yoga or other forms of Eastern meditation) is of only minor importance. It is the altered state of consciousness itself that opens the door to the occult—which the ancient yoga texts describe as being taken over by various Hindu gods.

In fact, both Stanislav through LSD, and Christina through Hinduism and yoga, were experiencing what they would only later learn was the "awakening of Kundalini, the serpent power." The connection between yoga and other facets of the occult—and the central role yoga plays—should be emerging for the reader by now.

The Power and Deception of Kundalini Yoga

In Chapter One, we saw how Yogi Bhajan was highly honored by Congress. It follows, then, from what we have just seen, that it was really Kundalini Yoga (which Yogi Bhajan introduced to the West) that the United States government unwittingly praised! His followers declare today:

Kundalini Yoga is the yoga of the Aquarian Age, and we are blessed to deliver it. As for the future, here's what our Teacher [Yogi Bhajan], the Master of Kundalini Yoga, has to say:

"Yoga with its every system is going to prevail. By the year 2013, forty to sixty percent of the people will be practicing yoga.... In the coming years, changes in technology, psychology, and sociology shall be huge. In this chaos of the information age it will be difficult for people to cope with their day to day lives. The body, mind, and spirit have to be organized to meet these challenges. The word is going to spread that 'Yoga is the way.' This ancient science has saved mankind before, is saving it now, and shall save it in the future."[13]

Obviously, those who believe they have found salvation in Kundalini Yoga have no need of Jesus Christ to be their Savior. Nor is there, according to the yogis, anything like heaven or hell in the future for anyone. Instead, human destiny is simply to escape the illusion of physical existence, of karma and the wheel of reincarnation, to realize that there is no sin, that punishment is not from a personal God for having defied His Law but from an impersonal force called "karma," and, in fact, that one *is* God and can create one's own universe with the Kundalini power realized through yoga.

The hope Yogi Bhajan sets forth of universal salvation sounds wonderful for those who ignore or are ignorant of God's Word. If true, it would certainly be a strong reason for everyone to begin to practice yoga. His grandiose claims are simply not true. Precisely when and how in history did yoga "save mankind"? There is no record of anything of that nature ever having occurred. If the yogi was so deluded about the past, what about his promises for the future? Could the yogis be promoting the very "doctrines of demons" concerning which Paul warned?

Investigating Kundalini

In response to the word "kundalini," Google has nearly 5 million entries—and more than 70,000 websites appear when one enters "dangers of kundalini"! There are, of course, thousands of warnings written by critics who advocate having nothing to do with either yoga or Kundalini. On one of them we read, "The author of this website has intimate and personal knowledge of the 'Kundalini Awakening' experience. If you explore the links on this site you will see that the experience is often debilitating, disabling, and sometimes life threatening. The experience can drive you literally insane and can continue for years."[14]

It is not only the critics, however, but the advocates of Kundalini by the hundreds if not thousands who likewise sound the alarm. Some of the strongest warnings come from those who have experienced Kundalini for many years, and who still advocate it, but who couple their encouragement to get into yoga with solemn reminders of its dangers. One Kundalini enthusiast writes:

> When the Kundalini awakens, tremendous power is unleashed. The resulting expansion of consciousness affects every element of our being, from our biological functions to our personal relationships to our concept of reality to our influence in the world. We are irrevocably changed in ways we could not have imagined and in ways we may never fully comprehend.
>
> For some of us, the risen Kundalini gives us our first or most unmistakable contact with the Spirit.
>
> Before my Kundalini rose, I thought the resurgence of Goddess religions was mostly a feminist backlash against millennia of a masculinized God. Now I understand it all quite differently. Kundalini is Shakti, the Great Mother

Goddess, the living energy that daily makes her vibrant presence known in my body and my psyche. She is as fierce and powerful as she is mysterious and enticing....

If Kundalini is to be invoked, it must be with care and better still, with reverence and humility. We are treading sacred waters here. To plunge in recklessly is to risk self-annihilation.[15]

Sacred waters? Again the spiritual side of yoga comes to the surface—and as part of the warning. *Shakti, the Great Mother Goddess* is the "living energy" awakened by Kundalini? This consort of Shiva the Destroyer is sometimes seen with her heel on his neck, apparently stronger and more to be feared than he. This is "goddess power" in action. Kali and Durga are some of her other names, and Hindus say "her beauty is in her terror"! A fitting description, indeed, of the Kundalini that yoga is designed to arouse within!

Warnings from Unexpected Sources

Even Swiss psychiatrist C. G. Jung, who was one of the earliest responsible for introducing Eastern mysticism to the West and was himself heavily involved in the occult, wrote:

One often hears and reads about the dangers of Yoga, particularly of the ill-reputed Kundalini Yoga. The deliberately induced psychotic state...is a danger that needs to be taken very seriously indeed...and ought not to be meddled with in our typically Western way. It is a meddling with Fate, which strikes at the very roots of human existence and can let loose a flood of sufferings of which no sane person ever dreamed...hellish torments....[16]

Yet Yogi Bhajan and other gurus who brought yoga to the West declare that Kundalini is the savior. If so, why should it be so dangerous to arouse it? And why should it be "ill-reputed"? Jung must have known something from his experience both in the East and as a psychiatrist that would cause him to issue such a warning. One can only wonder, then, why those who are drawn into yoga by advertisements concerning its alleged health and spiritual benefits are not given this kind of essential information. Is the truth (as is the immorality of the yogis) suppressed for commercial reasons?

It doesn't take much investigation to verify the fact that even after the dangers inherent in yoga and the evil of the yogis are known, their followers cover up the truth and continue to entice others to join their movement. Rare are those who tell the truth, such as in this stern warning from Puran Bair, American Sufi Master. Sufism is part of Islam. (Seyyed Hossein Nasr, one of the foremost scholars of Islam, in his article, "The Interior Life in Islam," contends that Sufism is simply the name for the inner or esoteric dimension of Islam.) Bair, who continues to teach yogic meditation, declares:

> There is a great danger in raising Kundalini in the first place: it may not turn off or the state it produces may become addictive. Having taught upward meditation for decades, I have seen many cases of aborted careers, broken marriages, dissociated psyches and neurological illnesses that I believe were caused by kundalini.[17]

With so much personal wreckage attributed to Kundalini, why would Bair or anyone else persist in pursuing it? Yet Christina Grof (founder of the Spiritual Emergency Network) claims that her life was transformed for the better by the arousal of her "kundalini." Convinced that this was beneficial, she writes: "My meeting with

Swami Muktananda really blew the lid off everything. He served as a catalyst to awaken what I had been resisting, which was kundalini (the universal life force)."[18] She apparently remains oblivious to the fact that yoga itself is a major source of danger and evil.

An Impressive Clientele

University professors and psychiatrists sat at Muktananda's feet in admiration and wonder—and more than one had his Kundalini allegedly awakened by this incredibly evil man. For example, consider the "shaktipat" experience of Professor Michael Ray of the Stanford Graduate School of Business, who was introduced to the Siddha Yoga of Swami Muktananda through his psychotherapist and came to a new view of human potential and its application to the business world. At that time, the Swami was the guru to many business leaders and Hollywood stars. Ray's life was transformed when an assistant to Muktananda ran a peacock feather across the "third eye" in the center of his forehead. Ray relates:

> I saw a bolt of lightning, like a pyramid of light. I began literally bouncing off the floor and trembling. I cried. I felt tremendous energy, love, and joy.
>
> What I had experienced, I later learned, had been shakti-pat, or spiritual awakening of kundalini energy inside me....[19]

Psychiatrist Gerald Jampolsky is famous for his use of *A Course in Miracles* in his psychiatric practice and in his books and lectures around the world. The *Course* was dictated by an entity that claimed to be "Jesus" but could not possibly have been. Jampolsky believes he was prepared for the message of the *Course* through *shaktipat* adminis-tered by Muktananda with a mere touch:

> It seemed as though I had stepped out of my body and was looking down upon it. I saw colors whose depth and brilliance were beyond anything I had ever imagined.
>
> I began to talk in tongues. A beautiful beam of light came into the room and...I was filled with an awareness of love unlike anything I had known before.... When I started reading the *Course*, I heard a voice within saying, "Physician, heal thyself; this is your way home," and there was a complete feeling of oneness with God and the Universe.[20]

A love "unlike anything I had known before"? Unquestionably, there was a "power" of some kind in Muktananda that convinced multitudes. One remembers the awakening from this delusion by a former follower. Troubled that he had been so deceived, he asked himself in bewilderment how Muktananda could be "both a saint and a devil at the same time"!

We can prove by irrefutable evidence from archaeology, history, and hundreds of prophecies fulfilled that the Bible is one hundred percent true in all that it tells us about God and the way of salvation through Jesus Christ. Jampolsky's experience of "oneness with God" through the magic touch of an undeniably wicked guru was the very antithesis of what the Bible teaches of God and reconciliation of sinners to Himself through the sacrifice of Christ on the Cross.

I well remember interviewing a former drug user who was on his way to becoming an accomplished yogi. Close to reaching "enlightenment" while high on yoga, he was confronted by the universe with which he desired "oneness." It appeared to him as the most beautiful woman he could ever have imagined, offering sexual union as the ultimate good. At that moment, an indescribable terror came over him. He cried out to Jesus Christ, who rescued him from drugs, yoga, and the accompanying delusions.

Shaktipat and "Slaying in the Spirit"

As previously mentioned, there are hundreds of warnings written by critics who, like this author, advocate having nothing to do with Kundalini. Of greater interest, perhaps, are the hundreds if not thousands of caveats by *advocates* of Kundalini. Some of them have experienced it for many years, yet they nevertheless offer some of the most severe warnings.

The experiences of Michael Ray and Gerald Jampolsky, like those of so many others whose Kundalini has been awakened, were much like the delusion that has convinced thousands of charismatics that they have received a "special touch from the Holy Spirit" through Kathryn Kuhlman or at a Benny Hinn "miracle" service. The same phenomenon has been reported at the former Toronto Airport Vineyard, as well as at the worldwide "revival" (now barely a sputter) that at one time flowed out of the Brownsville Assembly of God in Pensacola, Florida—or from the numerous other televangelists and faith healers who act in the name of Jesus but disobey His word in the process. One cannot escape the similarity between *shaktipat* and what the charismatics, both Catholic and Protestant, call being "slain in the Spirit."

At the touch of the evangelist, usually on the forehead, the subject falls backward into the arms of "catchers" standing by. In this trancelike state, he has a variety of occult experiences, from flashes of light to a sense of well-being and love; from uncontrollable weeping or laughter and violent shaking to "speaking in tongues." Evangelist and healer Kathryn Kuhlman made "slaying in the Spirit" a household term among charismatics in the '60s and '70s. Televangelist Benny Hinn claims to be Kuhlman's successor, having picked up "the anointing" from visits to her grave, which he says still lingers there. The "charismatic" experiences received from televangelists are scarcely distinguishable from the Kundalini arousal bestowed by a guru.

The author, although believing in miracles for the present (God and His power have not changed), rejects the unbiblical performances of today's pretenders and has exposed them in other books.[21] It has only been appropriate in this volume to tell the truth about Kundalini in both its physical manifestations and spiritual effects. It is up to the reader to recognize and admit the obvious connection with certain extreme charismatic manifestations and to act upon the facts. We hope and pray also that many involved in yoga will consider very carefully the truth presented herein before the delusion has reached the point of no return.

1. http://robertcowham.com/kundalini/kundalini.html.
2. http://www.experiencefestival.com/kundalini_yoga.
3. http://www.abc-of-yoga.com/styles-of-yoga/kundalini-yoga.asp.
4. http://www.realization.org/page/doc0/doc0026.htm.
5. http://www.itisnotreal.com/practices.html.
6. Christina Grof and Stanislav Grof, M.D., *The Stormy Search for the Self* (New York: G. P. Putnam's Sons, 1992), 21-22.
7. Revelation 9:21; 18:23; 21:8; 22:15. The Greek word translated "sorcery" in the New Testament is *pharmakeia*, from which we get the word "pharmacy," or "drugs."
8. Grof, *Stormy*, 23.
9. Peter R. Breggin, M.D. and David Cohen, Ph.D., *Your Drug May Be Your Problem: How and Why to Stop Taking Psychiatric Medications* (Reading, MS: Perseus Books, 1999), 41, 43-47.
10. Grof, *Stormy*, 24-25.
11. Ibid., 11-12.

12. Ibid., 13.

13. http://www.kundaliniyoga.com/clients/
    ikyta/webshell.nsf/WebParentNavLookup/
    62DB48EF3856D82287256A090079DC7A?OpenDocument.

14. http://www.yogadangers.com/AbouttheAuthor.htm.

15. http://www.experiencefestival.com/a/Kundalini/id/35190.

16. C. G. Jung, Trans. R.F.C. Hull, *The Collected Works of C. G. Jung*
    (Princeton, NJ: Princeton University Press, 1958), 520. See also Jung's
    introduction to *The Tibetan Book of the Dead.*

17. http://heartseva.com/index.html.

18. Stan and Christina Grof, "Spiritual Emergencies," *Yoga Journal*, July-
    August 1984, 40.

19. Bill Thomson, "Spiritual Values in the Business World," *Yoga Journal*,
    January-February 1988, 52.

20. Bill Friedman, Ph.D., "Interview with Gerald Jampolsky, M.D.," *Orange
    County Resources*, 3, from Jampolsky's book, *Teach Only Love.*

21. Dave Hunt, *Occult Invasion* (Eugene, OR: Harvest House Publishers,1998);
    Dave Hunt and T. A. McMahon, *The Seduction of Christianity* (Eugene, OR:
    Harvest House Publishers, 1985); Dave Hunt, *Beyond Seduction* (Eugene,
    OR: Harvest House Publishers, 1987); Dave Hunt, *In Defense of the Faith*
    (Eugene, OR: Harvest House Publishers, 1996).

—8—

꓄OGA, REINCARNATION, AND TRUTH

What are the real fruits of yoga? What does it do to the person who devotes his life to it? We have tried to show both sides of the coin. Those who are still caught in yoga's clutches will tell how wonderful it is because they want to believe it. Their lives would be shattered if they were to face the truth. Those who have escaped from yoga's grip, however, tell some horror stories. Here is one further example.

Raised a Hindu, the son of a "holy man" who was worshiped as a god, Rabi Maharaj followed in his father's footsteps, became a yogi at a young age, and he, too, was worshiped as a god by his followers. After spending hours in yoga each day for many years, he discovered that the Hindu deities he worshiped were trying to destroy him. Turning to Christ as the One who had paid the penalty for his sins, he escaped the Hindu/yoga deities. His reaction when he came to the West is interesting and instructive:

> I [have] observed with deep concern the rapid acceleration of a powerful but largely unrecognized Eastern influence upon

the average Western mind. This invasion by Eastern religions has subtly but heavily influenced almost every area of Western society. Through the deliberate efforts of Hindu and Buddhist gurus such as Vivekananda, Aurobindo, Shri Chinmoy (who leads meditations at the United Nations in New York), and the very influential Dalai Lama, significant changes in Western thinking, beliefs, and lifestyles have been effected.

Literally millions of people have accepted Eastern presuppositions, including karma, reincarnation, and vegetarianism for religious reasons; and...millions more...have become personally involved in countless Hindu-Buddhist sects such as the Hare Krishna movement, the Self-Realization Fellowship of Yogananda, [Maharaji's] Divine Light Mission, Nichiren Shoshu, and numerous related Mind Dynamics groups, such as Silva Method....

As a former Hindu who began to travel widely throughout the West, I was astonished to observe that not only Rosicrucianism and Freemasonry have Hindu/Buddhist roots, but that almost every one of the established and respected Western sects, such as Christian Science, Science of Mind, Religious Science, and Unity is a syncretistic blend of Hinduism and Christian heresy. Even the American-born Mormon Church...is founded upon basic Hindu concepts, such as the belief in the pre-existence of the soul, a multiplicity of gods, and the teaching that godhood is the ultimate goal for humanity.[1]

Eastern Meditation-The New Panacea

The influence of Eastern mysticism to which Rabi Maharaj refers is pervasive in the field of psychology and in the world of academia. Harvard University has long been among the leaders in promoting the occult through psychic research. One of its projects involved experimentation with Buddhist monks' alleged psychic powers. The results have been convincing. For example, a Harvard film crew, dressed for the Arctic, set out in zero-degree-Fahrenheit weather from a 17,000-foot-elevation monastery, accompanying ten monks who wore only sandals and light cotton wraparound cloths. At 19,000 feet, on a rocky cliffside ledge, "the monks took off their sandals and squatted down on their haunches...leaned forward, put their heads on the ground, and draped the light cotton wrappings over their bodies." Harvard professor Herbert Benson reported:

> In this position, being essentially naked, they spent the entire night practicing a special type of gTum-mo meditation called Repeu.... A light snow drifted down over them during the early morning hours.
> No ordinary person could have endured these conditions. We're sure of that. Yet the monks...simply remained quietly in their meditative positions for about eight consecutive hours....
> Finally, at the...sounding of a small horn, they stood up, shook the snow off their backs, put their sandals on and calmly walked back down the mountain again.[2]

Paramahansa Yogananda attempted to explain such amazing abilities of certain monks: "Lord Krishna pointed out the holy science by which the yogi may master his body and convert it, at will, into pure energy. The possibility of this yogic feat is not beyond the theoretical comprehension of modern scientists, pioneers in an atomic age. All matter has been proved to be reducible to energy."[3]

In fact, there is no evidence that any atomic conversion of any part of a yogi's body takes place. If that were the case, yogis would not need to eat, drink, or sleep for days at a time and could duplicate the feats of Superman. Yogis have definite limitations far below the level of atomic energy. Although the feats at times seem amazing, the possessing demon is obviously limited in what it can manifest through a human body.

The scientists at Harvard and elsewhere have accumulated data revealing that something paranormal is going on. But science cannot explain it, because the source behind what is called psychic power is not atomic but demonic—a source that science can neither identify nor evaluate. Eastern meditation, especially that associated with yoga, has been credited with miraculous power and has become increasingly popular in the West. It is a wide-open door into the occult.

The Old "Shell-Game Switch"

The development of such apparently paranormal powers through "meditation" has opened the West to numerous kinds of yoga, Eastern meditation, and other forms of mysticism. That has created a great deal of confusion and assisted in the seduction of the Western world by many yogis.

It is essential to understand the vastly different meanings given to the word "meditation" in the West from the meaning in the East. Meditation in the West has always been synonymous with contemplation, or thinking deeply about something. Christian meditation involves seeking deeper insights into God's Word (Psalm 1:2), pondering God himself (Psalm 63:6), reflecting upon God's works (Psalm 77:12), and considering what our responsibility is and what our response should be (1 Timothy 4:15; 1 Peter 3:15).

In contrast, Eastern meditation associated with yoga (in spite of Robert Schuller's naïve endorsement) involves *ceasing to think* and *emptying the mind*. It opens the door to demonic possession. By repeating over and over a word or phrase (a mantra), or focusing on a candle, the tip of one's nose, or upon one's breathing in yogic relaxation, the mind is emptied of rational thought and one enters an altered state of consciousness. An Eastern meditation instructor tries to promote this induced state as natural:

> If you're new to [Eastern] meditation, remember that all of us naturally meditate. We have ordinary experiences... that regularly put us in a meditative state: watching the sun as it sets, listening to soothing music, or just being at the water's edge.
>
> Our mind slows down, our body relaxes, and our consciousness changes. Our brain shifts into the slower frequency known as the alpha state. And that's it—we are meditating.[4]

What he describes is, of course, the opposite of the contemplation that meditation in the West has always involved. The Bible refers often to *eating* or *feeding* upon God's Word. This is also called *meditating* on God's Word. Of the fruitful man, the first Psalm says, "In his [God's] law doth he meditate day and night." Of course to feed, or meditate, upon God's Word means to think deeply about it in an effort to understand and gain greater insights. But in Eastern meditation, one is forbidden to think. The mind must become blank. Calling that "meditation" introduces a new meaning for a common word. The switch has been made and the West has taken the bait.

Turning to the East

Professional basketball coach Phil Jackson, who has won nine NBA titles, rejected biblical meditation and turned to the East. As previously mentioned, he involved the entire Chicago Bulls team in Eastern meditation, a practice he had picked up in college. He wrote, "The first time we practiced meditation, Michael [Jordan] thought I was joking. Midway through the session, he cocked one eye open and took a glance around the room to see if any of his teammates were actually doing it. To his surprise, many of them were."[5] Of course, with Jackson's success, many others wanted to get involved in Eastern meditation, hoping it would have the same results for them.

Jackson's turning to the East, including American Indian mysticism (all occultism is basically the same), resulted in his rejection of Christianity in which his parents raised him. His mother had put the words of John 3:16 on his bedroom wall: "For God so loved the world, that he gave his only begotten Son, that whosoever believeth in him should not perish, but have everlasting life."

Jackson didn't find what he wanted in Christ. He explains what he found in yogic Eastern Mysticism:

> What appealed to me about Zen was its emphasis on clearing [emptying] the mind.... One of the fundamental tools for doing that is a form of sitting [yogic] meditation known as *zazen*. The form of *zazen* I practice involves sitting completely still on a cushion with eyes open but directed downward and focusing attention on the breath.... Over time your thoughts calm down...and you experience moments of *just being* without your mind getting in the way...keeping your mind open and directing it at nothing.[6]

He is advocating the abandonment of rational control of one's mind and the opening of it to the influence of other minds. God does not honor such a state of mindlessness. That fact leaves only one other source for this power.

Buddhism offered Jackson an escape from the God of the Bible whom, as a young boy, he had once feared and had desired to please. Says John Daido Loori, abbot of Zen Mountain Monastery in upstate New York: "Buddhism is a...religion without a God or (depending on the school) an afterlife.... [It is] the search for the nature of the self, which ends in the realization that there is no self, that all the beings and objects...are manifestations of the same underlying reality."[7]

It requires very little common sense to realize the folly of such a belief. Of course, every *physical* thing (from microbes to plants to human bodies and brains) is composed of energy. But the "self" (i.e., the thinking soul, spirit, mind) is not physical, and has nothing to do with energy. Human beings and physical objects do *not* have "the same underlying reality."

In yoga, which comes from Hinduism or Buddhism (as we have thoroughly documented), one seeks to realize that the self is God. But what is the point, since in Hinduism, *everything* is God, and in Buddhism there is no God? If that is the case, then *nothing* is God. The very concept of "God" has lost its meaning. Therefore, to "realize" that the self is God, or that self is nothing (as in Buddhism), is basically the same. It's all just a mind game, anyway—an illusion called *maya*—so what does it matter? Consider the following from yoga and meditation teacher Ema Stefanova, a war refugee from Macedonia, once part of Yugoslavia:

> Yoga and meditation have been part of my life since early childhood in one form or another, and have given me tremendous strength at difficult times in my personal life....

I have been following my guru Paramahansa Satyananda's guidance filled with joy for over a quarter century....

Yoga is...often misunderstood...[it] has nothing to do with whether one can touch one's toes or not, or how far one can stretch one's physical form.... [I]t is more about evolution of consciousness, individual and collective [and living] in harmony with oneself and the environment, according to universal laws that apply to each and every human being.... Yoga has always been about an individual's journey, personally guided and nurtured by the everlasting relationship between guru and disciple....

Yoga in America has become yet another industry... yoga businesses are run by former businessmen who also pose as yoga teachers...with egos often bigger than those of the students....

The true yoga of today has relaxation and meditation as well as devotion at its heart...fasting, yoga cleansing, and practicing inner silence and meditation....

Thus yoga facilitates the transformation of consciousness...through the traditional practice of mantra, yantra, and mandala which comprise the very foundation of every traditional yoga and meditation system.[8]

The Delusion of Cosmic/Unity Consciousness

As already emphasized, a major goal of yoga is to reach "unity consciousness," also called "god-consciousness." Obviously, if God is all, then to reach the point of feeling a oneness with the universe and all that is in it is to have achieved the sense of oneness with God. This "unity" or "cosmic" consciousness is common on a drug high and is very appealing to those who have rejected a personal Creator.

This "consciousness" is a bit more difficult to reach by yoga. In contrast, however, to the delusion of a mystical union with an impersonal universe, the Bible invites everyone to personally know the God who created the universe and all therein. Christ's death and resurrection for our sins opened the door for God's love to be experienced in a personal relationship with Him by all who receive Him into their hearts.

Astronaut Edgar Mitchell, commander of Apollo 14, had the mystical experience of cosmic consciousness on his return trip from the moon. So profoundly was he affected that he abandoned the outer space program to explore inner space. He describes that experience and the transformation it made in his life in his book, *The Way of the Explorer: An Apollo Astronaut's Journey Through the Material and Mystical Worlds*:

> It wasn't until after we had made rendezvous...and were hurtling earthward...that I had time to relax in weightlessness and contemplate that blue jewel-like home planet suspended in the velvety blackness.... [I felt] an overwhelming sense of universal connectedness...an ecstasy of unity....
>
> We needed something new in our lives, revised notions concerning reality and truth. Our beliefs were, and still are, in crisis. It occurred to me that the molecules of my body and the molecules of the spacecraft itself were manufactured long ago in the furnace of one of the ancient stars....[9]

What do the material molecules of one's body, a spacecraft, and stars—none of which has or ever will have consciousness—have in common with one's conscious, thinking, intelligent soul and spirit? To fail to distinguish between inanimate matter and consciousness and personality is a delusion of colossal proportions. Mitchell had become a Hindu, though he might not acknowledge that fact.

Carl Sagan had the same philosophy. Like Mitchell, the best destiny he could hold out to mankind was that someday the molecules of their bodies might become part of a distant star system. Sagan was a pagan who worshiped the cosmos. He declared, "If we must worship a power greater than ourselves, does it not make sense to revere the Sun and stars?" Of course, it makes no sense at all. Jackson, Mitchell, Sagan, and others like them, prove the old saying, "Those who refuse to believe in and worship the true God will believe in anything."

Fantasies from "Inner Space"

The irrationality of Mitchell's experience of unity consciousness was overlooked in his delight at having achieved the Hindu's "*savikalpa samadhi*—a recognition of the unity of things while still perceiving them as separate."[10] Many people within the Christian church are having equally powerful mystical experiences that have brought them into occult delusion and bondage. Like Phil Jackson, Edgar Mitchell was raised in a devout Christian home. Jackson's was Pentecostal, Mitchell's was Southern Baptist. But neither man understood true Christianity, and thus each rejected his own misconceptions rather than the truth.

Returning from the moon, with his experience of *samadhi* fresh in his memory, Mitchell founded the Institute of Noetic Sciences, "dedicated to advancing our understanding of consciousness...."[11] He writes:

> I would like to close with a saying that those of you who have heard me speak have heard many times in the past. It helps me convey the notion that seems to be permeating

our thinking at this point.... It is that "God sleeps in the
minerals, awakens in plants, walks in animals, and thinks
in man."[12]

"*Our* thinking"? It is astonishing that *anyone* could believe in a
"God" who originally had no consciousness but who "awakened" in
plants and was finally able to think in man. Man's thoughts, from base
trivialities and petty selfishness to grandiose delusions and the monstrous evil of a Himmler or Hitler, do not reflect well upon Mitchell's
"God" who is not only everything but apparently everyone as well!

Once a professing Christian, Mitchell has even exceeded the
pagans by attributing evil thoughts, lusts, and wickedness to his
god who "thinks in man." Such is the deluding power of mystical
experiences (whether on drugs or through yoga) in furthering the
planned transformation of the West.

A Choice to Make

Why do we provide so much background information in this book,
so much emphasis on the larger picture, and such an effort to
identify so fully the invasion of Eastern mysticism that the West has
been increasingly embracing in recent years? It is vital to untangle
the threads that hold together yoga, Hinduism, Eastern meditation,
chanting, breathing disciplines, and the physical positions and
movements that both derive from and provide support for all these
aspects of Eastern mysticism and Eastern religions. It simply isn't
possible to separate them into component parts, which partially
explains why we Westerners entertain so much confusion about
what the word "yoga," all by itself, really means.

To clarify one more time: yoga is sold in the West as science, but it is in truth religion. It is promoted in the West as beneficial to health, but in the East it is a technique for dying. Yoga is a Sanskrit word that means "yoking" and refers to union with Brahman, the chief god in Hinduism. Thus, yoga's ultimate goal is to reach *moksha*, allegedly escaping the world of illusion (*maya*) of time and sense into liberation from the endless cycle of birth and death and rebirth through reincarnation.

The latter is another of Satan's appealing lies, which deceitfully appears to offer endless chances to "get it right the next time." Reincarnation is irrational, as we shall see. It defies common sense while simultaneously denying God's declaration that it is "appointed unto men once to die" (Hebrews 9:27).

Mantras play a major role in yogic meditation. There are Christians who imagine "Jesus" can be a "Christian mantra" to be repeated over and over. No! That leads to mindlessness. Any mantra (like the Catholic rosary) violates Christ's command, "use not vain repetitions, as the heathen" (Matthew 6:7). Making a mantra out of His name is thus doubly wrong.

Whatever mantras might be substituted by "Christian yoga teachers," the fact remains that *true* yoga mantras are the names of Hindu gods. Furthermore, the ancient yoga teachers all declare that the repetition of a mantra is a call to the Hindu god it represents (i.e., the demon) to come and possess the meditator. I have personally interviewed people who became demon possessed through yoga and have heard the heartrending stories of countless others who, though not possessed, have been led into spiritual destruction. The ancient yogis all warn of the grave dangers involved in yoga—warnings that are avoided by most Western yoga instructors.

This entire discussion always brings us back to the most fundamental fact about yoga. *No matter what physical benefit might be derived from the exercises themselves, yoga inevitably involves Eastern meditation.* And Eastern meditation, unlike Western *contemplation* or *reflection*, accompanies an intentional dissociation from our conscious minds. This shutting down of the mind is, in fact, a total abdication of our God-given responsibility that Jesus declared is the first and great commandment: to love Him with all our heart, soul, and mind (Deuteronomy 6:5–6, Matthew 22:37). Thus, we are violating one of the true God's most basic commandments every time we give our minds over to the intentional "nothingness" of yoga and associated "relaxation techniques."

Yoga is dangerous. Yoga is deceitful. The "correct" pursuit of yoga is designed to call upon demonic power and influence; it invites inside us the very separation from God and ultimate destruction it claims to forestall. Yoga is not good for anyone; clearly it is not acceptable for Christians.

The Delusion of Reincarnation

Another facet of yoga is its intimate relationship to the theory of reincarnation. Yoga was developed specifically as a hoped-for means of escaping endless deaths and rebirths. To this end, it has been practiced by Hindus, Buddhists, and others in the far East for thousands of years. In the West, many who were never deceived by the theory of reincarnation before have become intrigued by it and, eventually, have become believers as a result of their involvement in yoga. In Eastern mysticism, as in Christian Science, Religious Science, and other mind science cults, death, like life itself, is an illusion that can be overcome in the mind. Existence is simply an endless dream of birth, death, and rebirth through reincarnation.

Continuing Satan's lie to Eve that she wouldn't really die, the theory of reincarnation is continually promoted by the deceiving spirits "channeling" to mankind. This pagan theory's irreconcilable conflict with the Bible is clear. Scripture makes the uncompromising declaration: "...it is appointed unto men *once* to die, but after this the judgment" (Hebrews 9:27). Christ referred to two resurrections: "the resurrection of life" and "the resurrection of damnation" (John 5:29). Concerning the latter, we read, "I saw the dead, small and great, stand before God; and...the dead were judged...according to their works.... And whosoever was not found written in the book of life was cast into the lake of fire" (Revelation 20:12-15). There is no second chance.

In reincarnation, there are thousands of "second chances" in as many different bodies, male and female. Real Hinduism, of course, teaches downward as well as upward reincarnation: bad karma can drop one into the animal kingdom (or, in some cases, even the vegetable kingdom). This belief created the law of nonviolence (*ahimsa*): one must not step on an ant for fear it might be an aunt, or eat a chicken or any other creature for fear that it could be a relative working off "bad karma." Buddha, who practiced strict nonviolence, was unaware that in boiling the water for his tea, he was killing millions of living creatures.

This "real" reincarnation is generally not accepted in the West. Nevertheless, even there it is a continual struggle to pay off bad karma, build up good karma, and rise higher on the evolutionary scale. There is no such thing as resurrection but a "transmigration of souls" into one body after another.

Hinduism contradicts the Bible with an appealing lie that undermines the faith even of many professing Christians. They try to convince themselves that somehow reincarnation and resurrection can be reconciled. Many have even concluded—in defiance of Scripture—that it doesn't matter. There is no question, however, that the Bible teaches resurrection, not reincarnation.

It should be obvious that one cannot believe in both reincarnation and resurrection. The two are mutually exclusive—both cannot be true. In reincarnation, there is no conquest of death, but it remains victor. Each transmigration of the soul leaves one more body discarded and in the grave forever, death's eternally vanquished victim. In contrast, for those who believe on Him, the Bible promises complete victory over death through Christ's sacrificial death and resurrection for our sins. Scripture declares:

> ...the trumpet shall sound, and the dead shall be raised incorruptible, and we shall be changed. For this corruptible must put on incorruption, and this mortal must put on immortality. So when this corruptible shall have put on incorruption, and this mortal shall have put on immortality, then shall be brought to pass the saying that is written [in Isaiah 25:8], Death is swallowed up in victory.
>
> O death, where is thy sting? O grave, where is thy victory? The sting of death is sin; and the strength of sin is the law. But thanks be to God, which giveth us the victory through our Lord Jesus Christ. (1 Corinthians 15:52-57)

Jesus Christ was resurrected, not reincarnated. So will be all those who accept His death as payment for their sins and who die before the Rapture. Of course, those who "are alive" at that time "shall be caught up together with them [the resurrected believers]... to meet the Lord in the air" (1 Thessalonians 4:17). Antichrist, lacking the marks of Calvary, yet pretending to be Christ, will likely claim to be the latest reincarnation of the "Christ spirit."

An Appealing Lie Sweeping the West

Reincarnation has become a widely accepted belief in the West, promoted as offering an opportunity for additional lifetimes, one after the other. In the Eastern world, where it was invented, however, reincarnation is viewed as essential for working off bad karma accumulated in one's present and past lives. It is, in fact, understood as a means of punishment in kind in "next life" after "next life" for misbehavior in "past lives." The relationship to the Serpent's "thou shalt not surely die" is undeniable. Instead of dying, one is "recycled" endlessly.

The law of karma is impersonal and thus inexorable and without sympathy or mitigation, for which it has no provision or capacity. Consequently, there is no way to obtain forgiveness. One must suffer in the next life the precise pain, loss, or evil that one has caused to others in prior lives. The penalty must be paid with no grace or mercy possible. Gandhi called it "a burden too great to bear"—returning again and again to this life of suffering and disappointment, spinning forever upon a never-ending "wheel of reincarnation"!

Professing Christians go to astonishing lengths in attempting to reconcile the anti-Christian and Hinduistic theory of reincarnation with the Bible and even to find it "taught" there. Elijah is a favorite because "Malachi prophesies the return of Elijah, and Jesus says John the Baptist is Elijah returned."[13] Yet Elijah was taken to heaven without dying and appeared with Moses in conversation with Jesus (Matthew 17:3). Therefore, he could not have been reincarnated into John the Baptist's body, as it is claimed. Clearly, John the Baptist came "in the spirit and power" of Elijah (Luke 1:17), but was not Elijah himself in another body.

Yet some of those who teach reincarnation dare to pose as born-again Christians. Reincarnationist Herbert Bruce Puryear says, "I love Jesus, and I know Him as my personal Savior."[14] He contends, however, that "most of Christian theology must be reexamined and rewritten in the light of this new truth [of reincarnation]." How can he call himself a "Christian" when he follows another "truth" that contradicts the Word of Christ, who is *the truth* (John 14:6)? It is not surprising that Puryear, who does not base his beliefs on God's Word alone, has experienced in prayer and been deceived by "the radiant white light"[15]—so common in the occult—which has led multitudes of others to eternal destruction.

Reincarnation and Scientific Evidence

Yes, some scientific evidence is claimed for reincarnation. There are the studies of clinical psychologist Helen Wambach. She hypnotically regressed hundreds of subjects into "past lives" and found them to be more than 99 percent accurate in describing culture, living habits, and surroundings at the alleged places and times they claim to have lived in prior lives. Hypnosis, however, involves a highly suggestible state in which one is controlled by the hypnotist. It is entirely reasonable to believe that a demon could take advantage of this passive state to interject its influence upon the subject's passive mind as well.

Hypnosis is one of the oldest occult practices. No one should ever submit to hypnosis. In fact, most courts of law in the United States will not accept testimony from a person whose "memories" have been "uncovered" by hypnotic regression. Nevertheless, many Christian psychologists use hypnosis in counseling in order to probe into the patient's past. In contrast, Paul declared, "Forgetting those things which are behind, and reaching forth unto those things which are before, I press toward the mark for the prize of the high calling of God in Christ Jesus" (Philippians 3:13-14).

Another respected researcher in this area is psychiatrist Ian Stevenson. He has investigated and documented a number of cases of young children who, in the process of spontaneously expressing memories of past lives, gave so much factual data that there seemed to be no other explanation except reincarnation. Once again, of course, a demon could have provided such "memories" of past places and events. The demon would have observed people and events long ago, and could have gained control through the vulnerable hypnotic or passive state, using the subject's vocal mechanism to express, in the victim's voice, information it knows from the past. Thus, to observers, it seems that the victim of possession (which could be only temporary while under the hypnotic trance) actually lived and experienced these past places and events.

The dominance of materialism—which is the official state religion in the Western world—requires that in the scientific evaluation of the data, the possibility of temporary demonic take-over in an altered state is not even considered. Nor is there any way by materialistic science to know whether a demon was involved. Yet that possibility alone is sufficient to undermine the very rare examples reincarnationists can offer.

Reincarnation can be refuted by simple logic. Moveover, the Bible, which contradicts reincarnation, is fully verifiable in every point (see *In Defense of the Faith* by this author). One cannot believe in Christ's death, burial, and resurrection for the sins of the world and at the same time believe in reincarnation. To call oneself a Christian while believing in reincarnation is a monstrous contradiction. But let us look at this ancient pagan belief by pure logic.

Amoral, Senseless, and Hopeless

Even without reference to the Bible and Christianity, common sense indicts the theory of reincarnation as *amoral*, *senseless*, and *hopeless*. It is *amoral* because, far from offering any solution for evil, it actually perpetuates crime and wickedness. For example, if a husband beats his wife, the cause-and-effect law of karma will require him to be reincarnated in his next life as a wife who is beaten by her husband. And *that* husband will have to return in *his* next life as a wife beaten by *her* husband, and so forth, endlessly. In reincarnation, the perpetrator of each crime must become the victim of the same crime, thus necessitating repetition of the crime, with each successive perpetrator in turn becoming a subsequent victim at the hands of yet another criminal, who must in his turn suffer the same fate, ad infinitum, ad absurdum.

Reincarnation is also *senseless*. Why? Does anyone recall—without the deception of hypnosis—any of the endless number of past lives he or she has supposedly lived? Who remembers the mistakes made in "past lives" and lessons learned? Not one person in 10 million can testify to any benefit realized in the present life by remembering any of the alleged past lives supposedly lived.

Yes, there are some people who claim to have experienced a sense of *déjà vu* upon visiting certain places. But all the details of past lives' errors and insights as a help in the current life? Of course not! What, then, is the point of living again and again in different bodies and families only to bear the burden of bad karma due to misdeeds one can neither remember nor correct? It is argued that subconsciously we have such memories and are thus benefiting at an unconscious level. If that were true, we should see evidence that mankind has gradually progressed morally. Obviously, this is not the case. Modern man has been described as "a generation of nuclear giants but moral midgets."

History Exposes the Lie

As the media daily reminds us, instead of improving, the record left upon earth by each succeeding generation betrays declining morals, a rising rate of divorce, suicide, wars, murders, and drug addiction. No record of consistent improvement from one generation to the next can be shown, except in our ability to travel at ever-faster speeds and kill our fellows with greater efficiency.

Humanity's embarrassing record reflects just one aspect of the contradiction at the very core of yoga/Hindu thinking. Very few practitioners ever allow themselves to admit this fact, much less to address it honestly and directly. While science claims that man is evolving ever higher, archaeology records that the great Mayan, Aztec, and Toltec civilizations declined, as did Rome, exactly as is happening to the West. The claim that man is the result of hundreds of thousands of years of gradual advancement to an ever-higher order of being simply does not square with the facts. Mankind is not evolving upward but sinking ever deeper into decline—a decline that began with Adam and Eve and has continued ever since.

Evolution is the essential partner of reincarnation. There is no point in coming back after death again and again if no upward progress is being made. In Hinduism, out of which yoga was spawned, one allegedly moves from lower to higher castes if one's karmic record so warrants. Only when one attains the highest caste as a Brahmin—after who-knows-how-many setbacks along the way—may one then, through yoga, attain moksha and thereby escape further reincarnations. The Bible, however, says that man is degenerating into ever-more-immoral behavior. One need only study history to know which of these opposing views is correct.

Caught in the Net of Hopelessness

The fact that reincarnation, as well as being *amoral* and *senseless*, is also *hopeless* follows logically. The karma built up in the present life must be worked off in a future reincarnation. In that process, more karma is accumulated, which must be worked off in a subsequent life, and so it continues endlessly. The "wheel of reincarnation" that spins on endlessly offers no release. As for escaping through yoga, there is no explanation of how that practice could abrogate the immutable law of karma, nor any proof that anyone has ever effected such an escape.

A further moral dilemma is presented. It is axiomatic that suffering by an individual could never undo his past misdeeds. Nor could living a perfect life in the future (if that were even possible) ever expunge past wrongs or rectify the harm they have caused. Somehow, the just penalty must be paid or God himself could not forgive us. God's infinite mercy cannot void the righteous penalty His holiness demands for sin.

In recognition of these facts, Christianity alone provides the only possible means of forgiveness: the penalty for breaking God's laws is paid by God himself, who became a man through the virgin birth. Christ never ceased to be God, nor could He; and He will never cease to be man. Jesus Christ is the one and only God-Man, who, as perfect and sinless man, could represent the human race, and as God could pay the infinite penalty He has pronounced upon sin. Only on that basis can pardon justly be offered to all who repent and receive Christ as Savior.

What a difference there is between an impersonal law of karma, which can only perpetuate evil and suffering, and the personal God, who loves us so much that He became one of us to pay the penalty we deserved! Only by the full payment of the penalty demanded by God's holy justice could evil and suffering end—and only for those who accept Christ's payment in their place.

Those who reject Christ are doomed to pay the penalty themselves—which will take an eternity of suffering because the payment for rebellion against the infinite God can only be infinite. Such is the claim of the Bible (in contradiction to every man-made religion) and it is supported by hundreds of prophecies fulfilled, by conscience, and by common sense.

Eastern Mysticism and Ecumenism

Many Christians assure themselves that there is real virtue in trying to see all the good they can in everyone and that, in so doing, they are showing Christ's love. After all, doesn't the Bible itself in 1 Corinthians 13 state that love is the most important virtue? But love is meaningless without truth and justice. Instead of virtue, it would be wickedness to love evil. Showing the influence of Eastern mysticism, a recent poll revealed that 71 percent of Americans, 64 percent of those who claim to be "born-again," and 40 percent of self-described evangelicals do not believe in absolute truth.[16]

The deliberate denial of God's truth is promoted in all communications from entities claiming to be spirits of the dead, Ascended Masters, space brothers, "Jesus," or whoever is most appealing to the particular recipient. Judith Skutch, the publisher of *A Course in Miracles,* presents what "Jesus Christ" supposedly dictated to an atheistic psychologist. In what could hardly be a coincidence, the *Course* reflects the same promotion of Eastern mysticism that thousands have experienced on drugs, in hypnotic or yogic altered states, and which Edgar Mitchell embraced on his moon journey:

> The world you made...is only in the mind of its maker...by recognizing [this] you gain control over it.... The oneness of the Creator and the creation is your wholeness...your limitless power...it is what you are.
>
> God would never decide against you, or He would be deciding against Himself....
>
> Forgiveness...does not pardon sins...it sees there was no sin. All guilt is solely an invention of your mind...in understanding this you are saved...how simple is salvation! It is merely a statement of your true identity.[17]

This is Hinduism once again—a lie so obvious that it requires no refutation; but, sadly, its acceptance has created the superstition and suffering that has kept India in poverty for centuries. Every child has conscience enough to know that he is morally accountable for his deeds and that he is separated from God by his sin. Yet the lie is so appealing that intelligent adults by the millions embrace it in their desperate flight from truth and God. And the practice of yoga has brought many unsuspecting persons into the same delusion from the same source.

Physical exercise is necessary for a healthy body. Most people in today's world, particularly in the West, have jobs and a lifestyle that inhibit essential exercise. This fact requires that each of us must discipline ourselves to include in our daily lives some regimen of physical exercise. Yoga was not designed to provide the exercise vital for good health but for an entirely different purpose.

We have documented the purpose of yoga as intended by its originators. We have provided numerous examples of its evil effect in the duplicitous lies of the gurus who brought it to the West and who have been admired as exemplifying its virtues. We have shown that yoga is at the very heart of Hinduism and other forms of Eastern mysticism, and we have revealed its relationship to the twin lies of evolution and reincarnation. We have shown that yoga is in the fullest possible opposition to the Bible.

It is up to each reader to weigh the evidence, come to his or her own conclusions, and then act upon them in obedience to the truth.

But I fear, lest by any means,
as the serpent beguiled Eve through his subtilty,
so your minds should be corrupted from the
simplicity that is in Christ.

2 CORINTHIANS 11:3

1. Rabi Maharaj, *The Death of a Guru* (Eugene, OR: Harvest House Publishers, 1977).

2. Herbert Benson with William Proctor, *Your Maximum Mind* (Random House, 1987), 16-17.

3. Paramahansa Yogananda, *Autobiography of a Yogi* (Los Angeles, CA: Self-realization, 1971), 489.

4. Jonathan Ellis, "Practicing Meditation: Basic Techniques to Improve Your Health and Well-Being," in Deepak Chopra's *Infinite Possibilities for Body, Mind, and Soul*, October 1996, 4.

5. Phil Jackson and Hugh Delehanty, *Sacred-Hoops* (Hyperion, 1995), 11-12.

6. Ibid., 48-49.

7. Jerry Adler, "800,000 Hands Clapping," in *Newsweek*, June 13, 1994, 46.

8. Ema Stefanova, "Yoga and Meditation, from Macedonia to the United States," *The Crazy Wisdom Journal*, May-August 2005, 14-15.

9. Edgar Mitchell with Dwight Williams, *The Way of the Explorer: An Apollo Astronaut's Journey through the Material and Mystical Worlds* (Putnam, 1996), as cited in *Brain/Mind Bulletin*, August 1996, 4.

10. Ibid.

11. Undated letter from Edgar Mitchell on Institute of Noetic Sciences letterhead, 600 Stockton Street, San Francisco, CA 94108, (415) 434-0626.

12. *Noetic Sciences Review*, date unknown, 6.

13. Herbert Bruce Puryear, *Why Jesus Taught Reincarnation: A Better News Gospel* (New Paradigm Press, 1992), xii.

14. Ibid., v.

15. Ibid., v, xii.

16. http://www.pollingreport.com/religion.htm.

17. John Klimo, *Channeling* (Jeremy P. Tarcher, 1987), 149, quoted from Klimo's interview with Skutch.

Books by Dave Hunt

THE GOD MAKERS

—Ed Decker & Dave Hunt

Mormons claim to follow the same God and the same Jesus as Christians. They also state that their gospel comes from the Bible. But are they telling the truth? One of the most powerful books to penetrate the veil of secrecy surrounding the rituals and doctrines of the Mormon Church, this eye-opening exposé has been updated to reveal the current inner workings and beliefs of Mormonism. Harvest House Publishers, 292 pages.

ISBN: 1-56507-717-2 • TBC: B04023

DEATH OF A GURU:
A REMARKABLE TRUE STORY OF ONE MAN'S SEARCH FOR TRUTH

—Rabi R. Maharaj with Dave Hunt

Rabi R. Maharaj was descended from a long line of Brahmin priests and gurus and trained as a Yogi. He meditated for many hours each day, but gradually disillusionment set in. He describes vividly and honestly Hindu life and customs, tracing his difficult search for meaning and his struggle to choose between Hinduism and Christ. At a time when eastern mysticism, religion, and philosophy fascinate many in the West, Maharaj offers fresh and important insights from the perspective of his own experience. Harvest House Publishers, 208 pages.

ISBN: 0-89081-434-1 • TBC: B04341

THE SEDUCTION OF CHRISTIANITY:
SPIRITUAL DISCERNMENT IN THE LAST DAYS

—Dave Hunt & T. A. McMahon

The Bible clearly states that a great Apostasy must occur before Christ's Second Coming. Today Christians are being deceived by a new worldview more subtle and more seductive than anything the world has ever experienced. Scripture declares that this seduction will not appear as a frontal assault or oppression of our religious beliefs; instead, it will come as the latest "fashionable philosophies" offering to make us happier, healthier, better educated, even more spiritual. As the first bestselling book to sound the alarm of false teaching in the church, this ground-breaking classic volume still sounds a clear call to every believer to choose between the Original and the counterfeit. As delusions and deceptions continue to grow, this book will guide you in the truth of God's Word. Harvest House Publishers, 239 pages.

ISBN: 0-89081-441-4 • TBC: B04414

IN DEFENSE OF THE FAITH: BIBLICAL ANSWERS TO CHALLENGING QUESTIONS

—Dave Hunt

Why does God allow suffering and evil? What about all the "contradictions" in the Bible? Are some people predestined to go to hell? This book tackles the tough issues that Christians and non-Christians alike wonder about today, including why a merciful God would punish people who have never heard of Christ, how to answer attacks against God's existence and the Bible, and how to tell the difference between God's workings and Satan's. Harvest House, 347 pages.

ISBN: 1-56507-495-5 • TBC: B04955

THE NONNEGOTIABLE GOSPEL

—Dave Hunt

A must for the Berean soul-winner's repertory, this evangelistic booklet reveals the gem of the gospel in every clear-cut facet. Refines and condenses what Dave has written for believers to use as a witnessing tool for anyone desiring a precise Bible definition of the gospel. The Berean Call, 48 pages.

ISBN: 1-928660-01-0 • TBC: B45645

BATTLE FOR THE MIND

—Dave Hunt

Positive thinking is usually better than negative thinking and can sometimes help a great deal, but it has its limitations. To deny those commonsense limitations and to believe that the mind can create its own universe is to step into the occult, where the demons who foster this belief will eventually destroy the soul. Unfortunately, increasing millions in the West are accepting this mystical philosophy, forgetting that it is the very thing that has brought many deplorable conditions wherever it has been practiced. The Berean Call, 48 pages.

ISBN: 1-928660-09-6 • TBC: B45650

DEBATING CALVINISM:
FIVE POINTS, TWO VIEWS

—Dave Hunt & James White

Is God free to love anyone He wants? Do you have any choice in your own salvation? "This book deserves to be read carefully by anyone interested in the true nature of God." —Tim LaHaye, co-author of the *Left Behind* series. Calvinism has been a topic of intense discussion for centuries. In this lively debate, two passionate thinkers take opposite sides, providing

valuable responses to the most frequently asked questions about Calvinism. Only you can decide where you stand on questions that determine how you think about your salvation. Multnomah Publishers, 427 pages.

ISBN: 1-590522-73-7 • TBC: B05000

WHEN WILL JESUS COME?
COMPELLING EVIDENCE FOR THE SOON RETURN OF CHRIST

—Dave Hunt

Jesus has promised to return for His bride, the church. But when will that be? In this updated revision of *How Close Are We?* Dave takes us on a journey through the Old and New Testaments as he explains prophecy after prophecy showing that we are indeed in the last of the last days. In the process, Dave compellingly shows that Scripture illuminates the truth that Jesus will return two times, and that His next appearance—the "rapture" of His church—will occur without any warning. The question is, are you ready? Harvest House Publishers, 251 pages.

ISBN: 0-7369-1248-7 • TBC: B03137

COUNTDOWN TO THE SECOND COMING:
A CHRONOLOGY OF PROPHETIC EARTH EVENTS HAPPENING NOW

—Dave Hunt

At last, a book that presents in a concise manner the events leading up to the return of Christ. Dave Hunt, in his characteristic direct style, answers questions such as, Who is the Antichrist? How will he be recognized? How are current events indicators that we really are in the last of the last days? Using Scripture and up-to-date information, Dave draws the exciting conclusion that, indeed, time is short. This book instructs, encourages, warns, and strengthens, urging readers to "walk circumspectly, not as fools, but as wise, redeeming the time, because the days are evil" (Ephesians 5:15-16). The Berean Call, new paperback edition, 96 pages.

ISBN: 1-928660-19-3 • TBC: B00193

A WOMAN RIDES THE BEAST: THE ROMAN CATHOLIC CHURCH AND THE LAST DAYS

—Dave Hunt

In Revelation 17, the Apostle John describes in great detail the characteristics of a false church that will be the partner of the Antichrist. Was he describing the Roman Catholic Church? To answer that question, Dave has spent years gathering historical documentation (primarily Catholic sources) providing information not generally available. Harvest House, 549 pages.

ISBN: 1-56507-199-9 • TBC: B01999

WHAT LOVE IS THIS? CALVINISM'S MISREPRESENTATION OF GOD

—Dave Hunt

Most of those who regard themselves as Calvinists are largely unaware of what John Calvin and his early followers of the sixteenth and seventeenth centuries actually believed and practiced. Nor do they fully understand what most of today's leading Calvinists believe. Multitudes who believe they understand Calvinism will be shocked to discover its Roman Catholic roots and Calvin's grossly un-Christian behavior as the "Protestant Pope" of Geneva, Switzerland. It is our prayer that this book will enable readers to examine more carefully the vital issues involved and to follow God's Holy Word and not man. The Berean Call, 576 pages.

ISBN: 1-928660-12-6 • TBC: B03000

SEEKING & FINDING GOD: IN SEARCH OF THE TRUE FAITH

—Dave Hunt

It is astonishing how many millions of otherwise seemingly intelligent people are willing to risk their eternal destiny upon less evidence then they would require for buying a car—yet the belief of so many, particularly in the area of religion, has no rational foundation. With compelling proofs, this book demonstrates that the issue of where one will spend eternity is not a matter of preference. In fact, there is overwhelming evidence that we are eternal beings who will spend eternity somewhere. But where will it be? And how can we know? The Berean Call, 160 pages. [NOTE: This book is extracted from chapters in Parts I and II of *An Urgent Call*.]

ISBN:1-928660-23-1 • TBC: B04425

A CALVINIST'S HONEST DOUBTS: RESOLVED BY REASON AND GOD'S AMAZING GRACE

—Dave Hunt

Derived from material in the author's much larger scholarly work, *What Love Is This?* this "user-friendly" book was created out of the need for a non-intimidating, easy-to-read "introduction" to Calvinism. In *A Calvinist's Honest Doubts*, readers discover the heart of a Calvinist "seeker"—and the surprising result of his quest for truth in this fictionalized but true-to-life dialogue, based on years of actual accounts and conversations between the author and Calvinists, former Calvinists, those who love them both, and the Lord who bought us all. The Berean Call, 96 pages.

ISBN:1-928660-23-1 • TBC: B00193

JUDGMENT DAY!
ISLAM, ISRAEL, AND THE NATIONS
—Dave Hunt

In what is possibly the most comprehensive and clear-cut examination of ancient biblical prophecy and modern-day Middle East politics regarding Islam, Israel, and the nations, *Judgment Day!* is an eye-opening page-turner for scholars, analysts, pastors, professors, politicians, and laypeople alike.

Amazing historical facts and first-hand insight make this book a thrilling, sometimes troubling, read—but one that is necessary for an accurate understanding of the prophetic times in which we live. With painstaking clarity and detail, *Judgment Day!* reveals the ancient agenda against the Jews, and traces its twisted trail to modern-day deceptions of U.S. Presidents, foreign ambassadors, covert (and overt) military operations, businesspeople, educators, and world leaders alike.

In this no-holds-barred documentary, Dave Hunt skillfully dissects the myth of Palestinian claims to "the Promised Land," and exposes the fraud, deceit, and treachery of an international community allied against the Jewish nation. As the author writes, "In the final analysis, the battle over Israel is a battle for the souls and destiny of mankind. If Islam and the nations siding with her should accomplish their goal of destroying Israel, then mankind [from a biblical perspective] is eternally lost...."

Why are the stakes so high? What will the outcome be? Discover the uncomfortable but irrefutable truth in Dave Hunt's impassioned exposé—*Judgment Day!*

ISBN:978-1-928660-42-2 • TBC: B05858

AN URGENT CALL
TO A SERIOUS FAITH
—Dave Hunt

Have you ever prayed: Lord, how can I... deepen and defend my faith? • know and prove that God's Word is true? • share Christ with confidence? • refute false religions? • truly love God as He desires? • fulfill God's purpose for my life? • "rightly divide" God's Word? • understand Bible prophecy? • prepare for Christ's return? • understand and teach Bible doctrine?

The awesome sense of the greatness of God and the cosmic and eternal proportions of the work that He is doing seems largely absent from Christianity today. Could this be why so many carry the self-imposed burdens of man-made "programs" they are trying to put into effect in order to "live victorious lives" or to "advance the cause of Christ"? When we see that the task is totally beyond our capabilities, then we cease from our striving and begin to allow Him to work in and through us by His mighty power. Many would have us believe that self-love is the answer to the world's ills. Both Christian leaders and the unsaved are teaching and preaching this lie. In fact, it is self-love that has wrought the ills of the world: greed, lust, envy, and strife.

What we actually need is a passionate love for God and His Word, turning us from earthly ambitions to heavenly hope. Not even a kingdom ruled by Christ on this earth is our hope, but heaven itself. "Wherefore he saith, Awake thou that sleepest, and arise from the dead, and Christ shall give thee light. See then that ye walk circumspectly, not as fools, but as wise, redeeming the time, because the days are evil." (Ephesians 5:14-16)

ISBN:978-1-928660-33-9 • TBC: B00339

● ● ● ● ● ● ● ● ● ● ● ● ● ● ● ●

**The Berean Call (TBC) is a nonprofit,
tax-exempt corporation which exists to:**

ALERT believers in Christ to unbiblical teachings and practices
impacting the church

EXHORT believers to give greater heed to biblical discernment
and truth regarding teachings and practices being currently
promoted in the church

SUPPLY believers with teaching, information, and materials which
will encourage the love of God's truth, and assist in the
development of biblical discernment

MOBILIZE believers in Christ to action in obedience to the scriptural
command to "earnestly contend for the faith" (Jude 3)

IMPACT the church of Jesus Christ with the necessity for trusting
the Scriptures as the only rule for faith, practice, and a life
pleasing to God

A free monthly newsletter, THE BEREAN CALL, *may be received
by sending a request to: PO Box 7019, Bend, OR 97708; or by calling*

1-800-937-6638

*To register for free email updates, to access our digital archives, and to
order a variety of additional resource materials online, visit us at:*

www.thebereancall.org

BEND • OREGON